MATTHEW

PROCLAMATION
COMMENTARIES

● The New Testament
Witnesses for Preaching   Gerhard Krodel, *Editor*

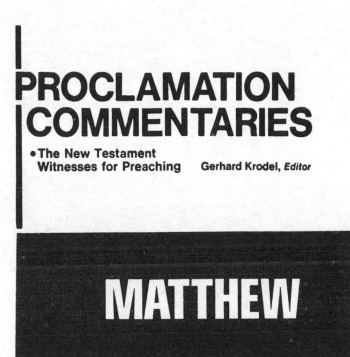

JACK DEAN KINGSBURY

FORTRESS PRESS   Philadelphia, Pennsylvania

Library of Congress Catalog Card Number 76-46732

ISBN 0-8006-0586-1

Fourth printing 1984

1457H84   Printed in the United States of America   1-586

To

Frederick & Lois Danker
Paul & Ruth Manz
Norman & Jeannette Kretzmann

"confessors" all

CONTENTS

The Gospel of Matthew has been called "the ecclesiastical Gospel." Its position at the beginning of the NT writings testifies to its esteem among the communities which shaped the canon. Since the days of the church fathers it has been the most quoted of the Gospels and its frequent use in the liturgy demonstrates its importance for the church. The Book of Common Prayer contained more lessons from Matthew than from Mark and John taken together. Its ecclesiastical character is also seen in that it is the only Gospel containing the word church (16:18; 18:17).

The favor in which this Gospel was held in the church was in no small way the result of the church's own legalism and of its belief that in distinction to Mark and Luke, the First Gospel was written by one of the twelve disciples of Jesus. The earliest tradition about its origin comes from Papias of Hierapolis who wrote about the middle of the second century: "Matthew wrote (collected) the accounts (logia) in the Hebrew language and each one interpreted them as he was able." However, an analysis of Matthew's language shows that the First Gospel is certainly not a translation from a Hebrew or Aramaic original. Moreover, source criticism reached the almost unanimous conclusion that the Gospel of Mark served as source for Matthew. If the first evangelist used a source which was not even written by an apostle, then apostolic authorship of Matthew becomes rather improbable.

Furthermore, form criticism pointed out that the content of Matthew's sources did not consist of one continuous eyewitness account, but rather of independent, separate narratives and sayings which originally had been transmitted orally. This implies that neither the First Gospel nor its underlying sources, Mark and Q, were composed by an eyewitness to Jesus' ministry.

Finally, redaction criticism focused its attention on the theological outlook of the author of this Gospel and concluded that he belonged not to the first, but to the second or third generation of Christians. We do not know why this Gospel bears Matthew's name. Perhaps his name became attached to this book because the community within which it was written was founded by Matthew, or perhaps parts of the materials had some connection with the erstwhile tax collector. The book itself is anonymous like the other Gospels. Its unknown author, whom we can continue to call Matthew, recedes behind the message which he wrote for his church.

What is the message of the first evangelist? This question has intrigued scholars since the nineteenth century and evoked quite a few different answers. More than once the first evangelist appeared to have been a Jewish Christian legalist, a sort of James among the Gospel writers. Bacon, in his *Studies in Matthew* published in 1930, saw this Gospel, patterned after the Pentateuch, proclaiming the new law of the new Moses. The importance of Matthew's ethical teachings frequently led to the neglect of the centrality of Christology in the First Gospel.

Jack Dean Kingsbury, Professor of New Testament at Union Theological Seminary, Richmond, Virginia, has been prominent in Matthaean studies during the last decade. It is not too much to state that he has given us a new interpretation of Matthew on a grand scale in which the nature and purpose of this Gospel are corroborated by its chief structural features and by its central theme. Its central theme in turn unifies Matthew's theology, Christology, and ecclesiology, and comes to expression in his understanding of salvation history, in his eschatology, ethics, his view of the law, of ministry, and mission. This book is easily the best interpretation of Matthew's theology today.

GERHARD KRODEL
Lutheran Theological Seminary at Philadelphia

AUTHOR'S PREFACE

It may be of benefit to the reader to know how this study relates to another book I have recently written on the First Gospel entitled *Matthew: Structure, Christology, Kingdom* (Philadelphia and London: Fortress and SPCK, 1975). Chapter one of that book deals with the broad structure of the First Gospel and with Matthew's concept of the history of salvation. Only a small part of that discussion has been reproduced here. Chapters two and three of that book are devoted to Matthew's portrait of Christ, and that material appears here in sharply curtailed form in the chapter on Matthew's understanding of Christ. The final chapter of that book, dealing with Matthew's concept of the kingdom of Heaven, has served as the source for the chapter in this volume on Matthew's understanding of God. Accordingly, where the two books overlap, the reader may wish to consult the earlier volume for a more extensive consideration of the topic in question. At the same time, fully half of the present book covers "new ground," especially chapter one ("Towards an Understanding of Matthew") and chapter four ("Matthew's Understanding of the Church"). Thus the two books also complement each other.

There have been few attempts in the last years to present a comprehensive overview of what may be termed the theology of Matthew. Perhaps the last major effort of this kind in English was B. W. Bacon's classic *Studies in Matthew* (London: Constable, 1930). It is my hope in the time to come to write such a volume, and my intention with this little book is to suggest some of the lines along which a theology of Matthew can be developed. Crucial in this regard is the way in which the central thought of the First Gospel is defined and its Christology, theology, and ecclesiology made to flow from it and to relate to one another. The contribution of this book to Matthaean research, as I see it, lies here.

Since 1973 it has been my pleasure to be a member of the Task Force on Matthew of the Catholic Biblical Association of America. I should like to take this opportunity to thank in print the other members of the group for the many insights into the thought of Matthew they have shared with me these last years. They are: Joseph A. Comber, O. Lamar Cope, Douglas R. A. Hare, Daniel J. Harrington, John P. Meier, Donald P. Senior, James M. Reese, and William G. Thompson. It is understood, of course, that none of them is responsible for the views advanced here. I should like also to thank my wife for cheerfully surrendering to the task of this book for a number of months her rightful claim to many week-end hours.

CHAPTER ONE

TOWARDS AN UNDERSTANDING
OF MATTHEW

The objective of this book is to treat Matthew's understanding of Christ, God, and the church. In the process the message of Matthew will also be delineated. This message, however, must be seen in context. To do this, we must have some idea of the nature and purpose of the Gospel. Is it, for example, of the nature of a history book that has been written to preserve for posterity a select number of revered facts? Or is it of the nature of a religious novel that is meant to inspire the reader? Or is it something else written for still a different purpose?

Theoretically, there are two ways to learn of the nature and purpose of Matthew's Gospel. The one is for us to attempt to cull such information from the writings of the early Church Fathers. This attempt has often been made, but without clear results. The second way is for us to study the Gospel itself. This is the course we have chosen.

Matthew's Gospel has been studied more carefully perhaps in the past hundred years than ever before. Especially since World War II, scholars have devoted an immense amount of attention to it, and great strides have been made towards gaining a better understanding of it. The goal of this chapter, therefore, is to probe the question of the nature and purpose of Matthew's Gospel with the aid of modern scholarship.

The Historical-Biographical Approach

Last century and in the early part of this century, the prevailing view of history was "positivistic" in nature. On this view the historian, through a critical reading of the ancient documents, endeavors to reconstruct the "facts" and describe "how things really were."

In the area of NT studies, one of the major preoccupations of scholars was the quest of the historical Jesus. The goal was to sift through the contents of the Gospels in order to establish an outline of Jesus' ministry according to time and place, and to determine both how he thought of himself and of his mission and what his teaching was concerning the kingdom of God. Because it was generally conceded that Mark's Gospel was the first to have been written, and because it furthermore seemed to contain primitive traditions, scholars quite naturally gravitated towards it as the most reliable source for historical-biographical data concerning Jesus. Conversely, they were much less inclined to involve Matthew and Luke in the quest, since the latter are more literary in character and appear to build upon Mark. Basically, they looked to them for sayings of Jesus Mark does not have. The result was that for a time Mark received by far the lion's share of scholarly attention, and Matthew and Luke receded into the background.

Still, during these years there were some scholars of note who stoutly defended Matthaean priority. They insisted that the First Gospel could be traced, if not directly then through the translation into Greek of an Aramaic original, to the hand of the apostle Matthew. Hence, it is the First Gospel, they maintained, that is in substance the earliest. In it one has access to eyewitness reports from the time of Jesus.

Not surprisingly, it was from among this circle of scholars advocating the priority of Matthew that the more imposing Matthaean commentaries came.[1] Moreover, it was within this circle of scholars that the so-called historical-biographical approach to the Gospel was also cultivated. We shall take up the question of the authorship of the Gospel in chapter four. But however this question is decided, the distinguishing feature of the historical-biographical approach to the First Gospel is the belief that the latter is of the nature of a chronicle, or documentary, the purpose of which is to present a relatively continuous and detailed account of events as they occurred in the life and ministry of Jesus.

As it was applied to Matthew's Gospel, then, the historical-biographical approach represents in effect an attempt to utilize the data of the Gospel to achieve the objectives of the quest for the historical Jesus. Indeed, appeal for this approach could even be made to the Gospel itself. The opening words, it was claimed, are to be translated "The Book of the History of Jesus Christ . . ." (1:1; cf., e.g., Gen. 37:2 [RSV]). These words, purported to be the title of the Gospel, were said to prove that it was Matthew's intention to write a "history book about Jesus the Messiah."[2]

Convinced that the First Gospel should be read as an objective report on the life of Jesus, the proponents of the historical-biographical approach attempted to draft a factually sound portrait of Jesus. In general, Jesus emerges in this portrait as the Prophet who proclaimed the gospel of the kingdom and as the Teacher who made known the will of God (4:23; 9:35; chaps. 5–7). Calling disciples to follow him (4:18–22; 10:2–4), he wandered about Galilee instructing and healing the people (4:23–25; 9:35). In order to gather from Israel a new community, he dispatched his disciples on a missionary journey (9:35–10:42). Owing to the fickleness of the crowds and the enmity of the Jewish leaders, Jesus recognized that only death lay before him (chaps. 11–12). Hence, he withdrew from public and embarked on private journeys with his disciples, preparing them for what lay ahead (chaps. 14–20). Finally, knowing that his time had come (cf. 16:21), he journeyed to Jerusalem, whereupon the events surrounding his death and resurrection took place (chaps. 26–28).

While there is perhaps nothing implausible about this outline of the life of Jesus per se, a prominent feature of the writings of those who have taken a historical-biographical approach to Matthew's Gospel is the great amount of space they devote to the filling in of the chronological and psychological gaps they encounter in the text. To illustrate this, consider merely two facets of the story of the temptation (4:1–11).[3] Thus, how is one to understand the circumstance that Jesus did not become hungry until *after* he had fasted forty days and forty nights (4:2)? This was the case, we are told, because during this time Jesus was caught up in such a state of spiritual exhilaration that he was not susceptible to pangs of hunger. Or how exactly is one to conceive of the devil as *taking* Jesus to the holy city and *setting* him on the pinnacle of the temple (4:5)? Since the devil is a spirit, what happened, we learn, is that he momentarily took such control of Jesus' senses that he experienced dizziness and only imagined himself to be standing atop the temple. The point is, neither of these explanations has any basis in the text; both arise from an effort to construe the text as objective historical description.

The latter statement is tantamount already to an evaluation of the historical-biographical approach to Matthew's Gospel. What are we to make of it?

The overwhelming evidence is that none of the Gospels is of the nature of biography. They were not meant to be "literary archives." They do contain historical traditions that go back to the life and times of Jesus. But they are not to be thought of as though each were a string of "verbal photographs" taken by family or disciples during the course of Jesus' life.

A look at the text of Matthew substantiates this judgment. The first thing to observe is that it is precisely those details which to our way of thinking make for good biography which are in especially short supply. For example, we are not told in which year Jesus was born or in which year he died. Neither is any mention made of the location of his tomb. And nothing is said about the length of his ministry, which is also true of that of John the Baptist.

Other personal details are likewise not in evidence. Following the infancy narratives (chaps. 1–2), the years that separate the early childhood of Jesus from his baptism as an adult (3:13–17) are passed over in silence. We are left in the dark about the school years of Jesus, about his intellectual development, and about the formation of his character. No description is given of his person, and his habits, mannerisms, and "likes and dislikes" are not discussed.

Neither do we catch a glimpse of Jesus' life at home. The friends of his youth and his relatives find no place in the gospel-story, and even references to Joseph and Mary and to his brothers and sisters are theologically, not biographically, motivated (cf. chaps. 1–2; 12:46–50; 13:53–58). As an adult, Jesus is reported as moving from "Nazareth" to "Capernaum" (4:13), which is described as "his own city" (9:1), and it appears that he has a "house" there (cf. 9:10, 28; 13:1, 36; 17:25). But the text does not elaborate on these terse remarks.

Except for Peter and Judas at best, even the disciples, the closest associates of Jesus, do not stand out as individuals. A list of their names is given (10:2–4), and now and again special mention is made of "Matthew" (9:9), of "Andrew" (4:18), and of "James" and "John" (4:21; 17:1; 20:20, 24; 26:37). But beyond the notations that Matthew is a "tax collector" (9:9) and Andrew, James, and John "fishermen" (4:18–22), and that James and John seem also to have shared the ambitions of their mother (20:20–28), nothing certain can be said of any of the disciples.

If the Gospel tells us little of the disciples as individuals, it tells us next to nothing of the other characters that dot its pages. Most of these persons do not so much as bear a name, passing before us merely as "a leper" (8:2), "a centurion" (8:5), "two demoniacs" (8:33), "a paralytic" (9:2), "disciples of John" (9:14; 11:2), "a ruler" (9:18), "a woman" (9:20), "two blind men" (9:27; cf. 20:30), "a dumb demoniac" (9:32; cf. 12:22), "a Canaanite woman" (15:22), "a man" (17:14), "a child" (18:2), "the young man" (19:22), "a lawyer" (22:35), etc. Other characters are indeed introduced by name, but to all intents and purposes they, too, remain people without profile: "Peter's mother-in-law" (8:14), "Caiaphas" (26:3, 57), "Simon the Leper" (26:6), "Simon of Cyrene" (27:32), "Mary Magdalene" (27:56, 61; 28:1), "Mary the mother of James and Joseph" (27:56, 61; 28:1), and "Joseph of Arimathea" (27:57) (cf. also "the Magi" [2:1] and "the mother of the sons of Zebedee" [20:20; 27:56]).

Nor is it any different with the enemies of Jesus. Herod and Pilate stand out to some degree as personalities. But even the name "Herod" is deceptive, since the text leaves it up to the reader to distinguish between Herod the Great (chap. 2) and Herod Antipas (14:1–12). The leaders of the Jews, in turn, appear as stereotyped groups. They confront the reader most often as the "Pharisees," the "scribes," the "scribes and the Pharisees," the "Pharisees and Sadducees," or the "chief priests and the elders of the people." Outside the passion narrative, they arrive on the scene suddenly and most often without motivation, and vanish again just as quickly. And while the people among whom Jesus carries out his ministry are depicted as assuming a neutral or even a positive attitude towards him until his arrest (cf. 27:20–26, 39–40), they simply remain the anonymous masses throughout the Gospel, the "crowds."

Accordingly, a survey of the biographical detail of Matthew's Gospel by no means leaves the impression that it stems from historical reflection on the life of Jesus. How do things stand as far as the chronological and topographical detail is concerned?

Chronologically, Matthew marks the passing of time with a series of literary expressions that invite comment only because they are so vague and indefinite. Thus, in any number of passages it is the mere particle "and" that removes in time one event from another (cf. 4:23; 9:35: "*And* he went about all Galilee . . ."). In ninety instances it is the adverb "then," and frequently it is the circumstantial participle (cf. 5:1; 9:36: "And *when* he saw the crowds . . ."; 12:46: "And *while* he was yet speaking to the crowds . . ."). In still other passages it is the indistinct prepositional phrase that performs the same function: "from that time on" (4:17; 16:21; 26:16); "at that time" (11:25; 12:1; 14:1); "at that hour" (8:13; 10:19; 18:1; 26:55); "from that hour" (9:22; 15:28; 17:18); "on that day" (13:1; 22:23); and "from that day" (22:46).

Topographically, the various settings in which Matthew depicts Jesus as discharging his ministry are likewise bland and for the most part imprecise. We encounter Jesus, for example, at the "Jordan" river (3:13), in the "desert" (4:1), on "a [the] mountain" (4:8; 5:1; etc.), "beside the Sea of Galilee" (4:18; 13:1), in "their synagogue(s)" (4:23; 9:35; etc.), at "home" (9:10; cf. 9:28; etc.), in a "boat" (13:2), "on the way" (20:17), going on or withdrawing "from there" (4:21; 12:15; etc.), and "in the region(s)" of the Gadarenes, of Tyre and Sidon, of Caesarea Philippi, or of Judea across the Jordan (8:28; 15:21; 16:13; 19:1). Apart from the passion narrative and references to the dwelling in Capernaum, the most exact Matthew becomes in identifying any given setting is when he informs the reader that Jesus is in the "house of Peter" (8:14), in or near a particular city ("Bethlehem," "Capernaum," "Bethphage," "Nazareth," "Jericho," "Jerusalem"), in "the temple" (21:12, 23), or on "the Mount of Olives" (24:3).

The paucity of biographical detail in the First Gospel and the imprecise fashion in which Matthew operates with chronological and topographical data are in themselves a strong indication that Matthew himself has not approached his materials from a historical-biographical point of view. But hand in hand with these factors, there is also Matthew's blatant disregard of other matters that would be of importance in any historical-biographical approach to the Gospel. The following examples demonstrate this.

In connection with the missionary discourse (10:5b–42), which Jesus is described as delivering to his disciples in preparation of their journey to the "lost sheep from the house of Israel" (10:6), Matthew writes that he "sent out" the twelve (10:5a). Still, once Jesus has finished the discourse, Matthew says nothing whatever about the disciples' actually undertaking this journey about which Jesus had spoken to them at such length. Mention is made neither of their departure nor of their return. In Mark, by contrast, both departure and return are duly noted (6:7–13, 30). If Matthew saw it as his task to write a life of Jesus in the modern sense of the term, his procedure at this juncture is baffling. But suppose he is not writing biography. Suppose this discourse of Jesus and its setting are of significance to him because they are of theological relevance to the post-Easter church of his own day: they treat of the Christian mission directed first towards Israel (cf. 10:5b–6) and subsequently towards the nations (cf. 10:18) and of the trials this missionary church can always expect to endure and of the cost and reward of discipleship. But if Matthew's procedure in 9:35–10:42 is dictated by theological and not simply historical considerations, then it is perfectly comprehensible. He had no need to dwell on the departure and return of the twelve, because with the completion of Jesus' discourse he had made his point.

A second example has to do with Matthew's portrait of the leaders of Israel. Five times he makes reference to the "Pharisees and Sadducees" as to a single group (3:7; 16:1, 6, 11, 12). What is so striking about this is the fact that, in the days of Jesus, the Pharisees and the Sadducees comprised two distinct "parties" with sharply contrasting views and theologies. The Pharisees were progressive, a party among the people. Their goal was that Israel should become the righteous nation of the covenant, and to this end they taught compliance with the so-called "tradition of the elders" (cf. Matt. 15:2), a code of conduct that effectively adapted the law of Moses to later times and changing demands. The Sadducees, on the other hand, were a wealthy, conservative party that was concentrated in Jerusalem and made up of aristocratic families of patrician and priestly stock. They refused adherence to the Pharisees' tradition of the elders, advocated a rigorous application of the law of Moses to the life of the nation, and in general espoused a political and religious policy including cooperation with the Romans which was aimed at preserving the status quo. The question is, what has prompted Matthew to treat these two parties as one group?

This question cannot be answered satisfactorily on a purely his-

torical basis.   The reason is that Matthew's procedure in this regard
is, again, theologically motivated.   At 3:7 he has John the Baptist
call the "Pharisees and Sadducees" a "brood of vipers," and in 12:34
and 23:33 it is Jesus who applies this same epithet, respectively, to
the "Pharisees" (12:24) and to the "scribes and Pharisees" (23:27).
The point is this: Matthew is not concerned to distinguish historically, in terms of the days of Jesus, between particular factions of the
leaders of Israel; instead, they all have become for him representatives of a monolithic front that stands implacably opposed to Jesus
Hence, the way in which Matthew deals with Israelite leaders of
whatever stripe is governed by the theological dictum that they are
the epitome of this "evil and adulterous generation" (cf. 12:38–39;
16:1, 4).   Once this is understood, we can see why it is that the
"Pharisees and Sadducees" should present themselves in the First
Gospel as a single group.

   Matthew's intent to work theologically with traditional materials,
not just historically, furthermore reflects itself in his portrait of Jesus
and of the disciples.   Take, for instance, the manner in which people
address Jesus in the First Gospel.   In Mark, Jesus is called "rabbi"
or "teacher," equivalent terms of human respect, both by the disciples and those who come to him in faith (9:5; 10:51; 11:21; 4:38;
9:17, 38; 10:35; 13:1), and by the traitor Judas (14:45), a rich
stranger (10:17, 20), a scribe (12:32), and enemies (12:14, 19).
In Matthew's Gospel, on the contrary, only Judas, a stranger, and the
opponents of Jesus address him as "rabbi" or "teacher" (26:25, 49;
8:19; 12:38; 19:16; 22:16, 24, 36).   When his disciples or persons
of faith appeal to him, they do so as "Lord," acknowledging thereby
that he is one of exalted station who wields divine authority (cf., e.g.,
8:2, 6, 8, 21, 25; 9:28).   This careful differentiation between "believers" on the one hand and "outsiders" and "opponents" on the
other as regards the manner in which they address Jesus cannot be
squared with "things as they really were" in the life of Jesus; it
admirably shows how Matthew has reshaped earlier traditions in line
with the beliefs and experiences of his post-Easter church.

   A glance at Matthew's portrait of the disciples undergirds the truth
of this assertion.   Mark depicts them during the ministry of Jesus as
being "without understanding" and in this sense "hard of heart" (cf.
4:13; 6:52; 8:17, 21; 9:10, 32).   And both Luke and John stipulate

that it was not until the resurrection that the disciples were led to grasp the deeper significance of the person and ministry of Jesus (Luke 18:34; chap. 24; John 2:22; 12:16; 16:4).

From the witness of the NT, it is surely correct historically to say that the disciples did not perceive aright what had transpired in the life of Jesus until they had gazed upon this life from the vantage point of Easter. Each in his own fashion, Mark, Luke, and John attest to this circumstance. Matthew, however, flies in the face of it. He consistently pictures the disciples as persons who can understand. In principle, they have "eyes that do see" and "ears that do hear" the "mysteries of the kingdom of heaven" (13:11, 16:17; cf. 13:23, 51). Their ignorance is never more than temporary, until Jesus has had opportunity to explain the matter (cf. 13:36 with 13:51; 15:15–16 [note the word "still" in v. 16]; 16:9 with 16:12). How are we to account for this? The explanation is that Matthew has endowed the disciples before Easter with insight that, historically speaking, they did not attain until after Easter. Matthew has impressed upon the tradition the theological perspective of his church.

We have given four illustrations of the way in which Matthew works theologically with traditional materials. When we consider that the historical-biographical approach to the First Gospel rests on the premise that Matthew writes primarily as a historian endeavoring to compile for all time a chronicle of the life and times of Jesus, we recognize the fundamental inappropriateness of this approach. As we shall see, Matthew is highly respectful of the past. But he is first of all a theologian, writing for the church of his day. What this means, finally, is that he does not compose his Gospel as one whose goal is to repristinate the days of Jesus prior to the crucifixion, but as one who tells of the person, ministry, and passion of Jesus from the standpoint of post-Easter faith. But now we are encroaching upon the discussion to come.

The Redaction-Critical Approach

At the turn of the century, Johannes Weiss[4] and Albert Schweitzer[5] sounded the death knell of the liberal quest of the historical Jesus. By the same token, the single most important factor in overcoming the historical-biographical approach to the First Gospel was the rise of NT form-criticism following World War I. Redaction-criticism, which emerged as a distinct discipline following World War II, is in many respects an extension of form-criticism.

One of the chief contributions of the form-critics was that they called attention to the importance of the "situation-in-life" (*Sitz im Leben*) in the preservation and development of the gospel tradition. Subsequently, scholars have learned to distinguish broadly between three such life-situations.

The first has to do with the times of the earthly Jesus. Surrounded by his disciples, Jesus in the course of his ministry proclaimed the nearness of the kingdom of God, preached his message also in parables, instructed his disciples, performed miracles, engaged in debate with the leaders of the Jews, sat at table with tax-collectors and sinners, and went the way of the cross. To attempt to determine and to understand what Jesus said or did or what happened to him on any given occasion of his ministry is to attempt to place a word of his or a story about him in its first situation-in-life.

The second situation-in-life pertains to the years immediately following Easter when the church came into being and, in the expectation of Jesus' imminent return, proclaimed him to the Jews and then to the gentiles as the Christ crucified and raised. There is no evidence that Jesus ever left behind a written document. This means that in the aftermath of Easter it was up to the followers of Jesus to recall words he had spoken, deeds he had done, or events they knew had happened to him (e.g., his baptism, temptation, or transfiguration). What kind of words, deeds, or events did they recall, and to what end? To judge from the Gospels, the followers of Jesus recalled sayings and parables of his in which they knew him to be revealing his divine authority, or setting forth his message of the kingdom, or sketching the ethics of the kingdom, or describing the way of discipleship, or teaching his disciples to pray, or telling of things to come. As for his deeds, they recalled miracles he had performed, debates he had had, or other events that revolved around him.

What motivated the followers of Jesus to recall such sayings, deeds, and events? As a result of the Easter appearances of Jesus, his followers believed him to be alive and exalted by God to rulership. They understood him to be present in the circle of their community, presiding over it in the power of his Spirit. Accordingly, through the recollection of sayings of his and narratives about him they knew him to be interacting with them in their worship and guiding them in their preaching, teaching, life, and controversies with opponents. The vehicles for such remembering were quite simply "mind and mouth." Therefore the words of Jesus and the narratives about him, the "stuff" that makes up our written Gospels, can be seen to have assumed the form of an oral tradition. Then, too, since Jesus was indeed confessed to be alive, his followers furthermore believed that he spoke to them, not only through the recollection of past words and deeds, but also afresh: through new or adapted words for new and changed situations. Thus, from its inception the gospel tradition was not static but dynamic in character, for through it the living and reigning Christ was seen as communicating with his followers in ever different circumstances. To attempt to determine the form and meaning of a saying of Jesus or narrative about him in relation to the setting in which it was used in the worship, life, and mission of the early church following Easter is to attempt to place that saying or narrative in its second situation-in-life.

The third situation-in-life is associated with the age of the evangelists. Following Easter, the gospel tradition, we stated, was oral in form. At this stage, sayings and parables of Jesus and stories about him circulated among Christians independently of one another. In point of fact, long after certain portions of the gospel tradition had been committed to writing, other portions continued to be transmitted from one generation to another by word of mouth. Still, after a period of years the time came when a written tradition did begin to emerge. Although it is a debated issue, some scholars believe that the gospel-source dubbed "Q" is an example of an early, written document. It appears to have been a collection of sayings of Jesus interspersed with several narratives, dating from about A.D. 45 or 50. An unusual feature is that it seems not to have contained a passion narrative.

However we are to think of Q, the first written document that may be called a "Gospel" in the literary sense of the term is Mark (c. A.D. 70). Matthew and Luke followed some years later, and John was written last, at the end of the first century.

Redaction-critics direct their attention to the Gospels themselves. As regards Matthew, Mark, and Luke, the so-called synoptics, painstaking scrutiny reveals basic similarities and differences among them, both as to make-up and wording. The result is that each evangelist, in response to the peculiar needs and situation of his church, can be found to present Jesus in his own unique way. Although none of them approaches his subject matter as a modern-day novelist but instead binds himself to gospel traditions handed down to him, all nevertheless must be respected as genuine authors. On this point, redaction-critics take issue with their form-critical predecessors: whereas the early form-critics regarded the evangelists as mere editors, transmitters, or compilers of the gospel-tradition, redaction-critics speak of them as "author-personalities," as individuals who have worked creatively with the gospel materials at their disposal. At any rate, to attempt to determine the nature, purpose, and message of any given Gospel, as well as the situation that gave rise to it, is to attempt to analyze that Gospel in relation to the third situation-in-life. The present study on Matthew, therefore, is a study in redaction-criticism.

One more word on this method is in order. Although redaction-criticism did not attain the status of an independent discipline until after the Second World War, one should not imagine that there were not scholars between the wars whose work did not anticipate the redaction-critical approach to Matthew. As far as the interpretation of this Gospel is concerned, a continuum runs from the era of form-criticism to that of redaction-criticism.

Attempts at Defining the Nature and Purpose of Matthew

We learned above that Matthew is not of the nature of biography the purpose of which is to repristinate for future generations the life and times of Jesus. How have those who have taken a redaction-critical approach to Matthew assessed its nature and purpose?

If one looks at the First Gospel closely, one discovers in it the fivefold use of the following, stereotyped formula: "And it happened when Jesus finished . . ." (7:28; 11:1; 13:53; 19:1; 26:1). This formula marks the conclusion of five great speeches of Jesus and thus calls attention to them: the Sermon on the Mount (chaps. 5–7), the Missionary Discourse (chap. 10), the Parable Discourse (chap. 13), the Ecclesiological Discourse (chap. 18), and the Eschatological Discourse (chaps. 24–25). Furthermore, it is also striking that

Matthew should describe Jesus, in connection with his giving his first major discourse, as ascending the "mountain" to deliver it. In view of these factors, could it not be that the First Gospel is of the nature of a compend of Jesus' commandments arranged after the fashion of the Mosaic Pentateuch for the purpose of combating within Matthew's church the heresy of lawlessness?[6]

The schematic way in which Matthew has arranged his Gospel is apparent throughout. Might not the arrangement of the Gospel therefore indicate that it is of the nature of a lectionary[7] or catechism,[8] the purpose of which is, respectively, to provide Scripture readings for the church's services of worship or instruction for Christian converts?

In addition to the careful way in which the First Gospel has been composed, a consideration of matters of content that are most typically Matthaean in Matthew's treatment of the gospel reveals an emphasis on a broad range of subjects: ethics, apostleship, teaching about the kingdom, church discipline, and eschatology. Is it not compelling, then, to regard Matthew's Gospel as of the nature of a manual, the product of a school, the purpose of which is to aid teachers and church leaders in instruction and administration within the church?[9]

From another perspective, in the opening verse of his Gospel Matthew lends great prominence to the word "book." On the assumption that he employs this word to describe the entire document he writes, must not the First Gospel be held to be of the nature of a "book" the purpose of which is to highlight "sermons"[10] or the "new verbal revelation"[11] which Jesus mediates to the church of Matthew?

In other respects, the First Gospel reveals that Matthew has also reflected in depth on questions relating to the history of salvation. For example, he is greatly exercised by the problem of the church's relationship to Israel. In consideration of this, is not the Gospel to be construed as of the nature of a revised version of Mark, the purpose of which is to portray the church as the "true Israel" which has replaced the Jews, or "false Israel," who have forfeited their place in the history of salvation as God's chosen people?[12] Or, in variation of this, is not the Gospel to be regarded as of the nature of historical reflection standing in the service of preaching, the purpose of which is to counter doubt that God keeps his promises by asserting that he has in fact been faithful to his people throughout history and that in Jesus and in the church his promises are coming to fulfillment?[13]

But scrutiny of the Gospel reveals that the place of the law in the church is likewise of central concern to Matthew. If this is the case, is not the Gospel to be thought of as of the nature of a legal document, the purpose of which is to exhort the followers of Jesus in the time of the church to observe Jesus' normative interpretation of God's will over against both Pharisaic Judaism and Hellenistic antinomianism?[14]

Again, Matthew lives at a time that seems no longer to expect the imminent return of Jesus. Does not this suggest that Matthew has composed a "life of Jesus" with eschatological relevance and ordered it as the "way of righteousness" in the ongoing history of salvation?[15] Or what of the themes of the gentile mission or of the persecution of Christians, which also stand out so noticeably in the First Gospel? Is not the First Gospel to be seen as of the nature of a "life of Jesus" and "Acts of the Apostles" rolled into one, the purpose of which is to set forth the more recent history of salvation: the "pre-history of the Messiah," the "history of the call of Israel," and the "call of the gentiles"?[16] Or is it not rather to be seen as a document the composition of which has been governed by the experience of Matthew's church of internal dissension and of external opposition from the gentile nations?[17]

None of these redaction-critical attempts to specify the nature and the purpose of Matthew's Gospel can be lightly dismissed. All of them underline basic aspects of the Gospel which must be explained if Matthew's document as a whole is to be understood. Most immediately, however, the value of these attempts is that they stress the necessity of beginning an investigation of the Gospel by considering matters relating to its composition.

Questions Concerning the Composition of Matthew

An important question in dealing with the composition of the Gospel is whether Matthew the author is to be identified with Matthew the apostle (9:9; 10:3). In chapter four we shall discuss the authorship of the First Gospel in greater detail. But here it must be said that the evidence does not seem to indicate that Matthew the apostle was the author of the Gospel. For one thing, Matthew the author appears to have set Mark's Gospel at the basis of his work. According to one count, he has appropriated more than 600 of the 661 verses of Mark's text.[18] What is more, it appears that he has followed the outline of the Second Gospel.[19] Broadly speaking, in both of them Jesus discharges his ministry in Galilee, undertakes the journey to Jerusalem, and there suffers and is raised. If Matthew the apostle were Matthew the author, such dependence upon Mark, whom no one claims was an apostle or eyewitness of Jesus, is virtually inexplicable. Why did the apostle Matthew not draw from his own recollection of events? Hence, it is highly doubtful that Matthew the author should be identified with Matthew the apostle and thought of as an eyewitness to the events of the ministry of Jesus.

Some commentators attempt to circumvent this conclusion by suggesting that Matthew the apostle influenced the final shape of the Gospel in the sense that he was the author of the sayings-source Q or of a primitive Aramaic document that was translated into Greek and incorporated into canonical Matthew. But against the latter thesis stands the fact that canonical Matthew cannot be described as translation Greek. And whether Matthew the apostle had anything to do with Q is a moot point, since we are without means either to prove this assertion or to disprove it.

In view of the shape of the First Gospel, what prompted Matthew to revise Mark? The answer, to put it bluntly, is that Mark was no longer adequate to meet the needs of Matthew's church. This can be seen especially well in the areas of Christology, ecclesiology, and the history of salvation.

Thus, Mark presents Jesus above all as the Son of God and the Son of man. Matthew follows suit, but develops both categories more extensively. He also stresses to a greater degree than Mark the notion that Jesus Messiah, the Son of God, is the exclusive teacher of his church (cf. 5:1–2; 23:8–10; 28:20). In other respects, Matthew furthermore transforms Mark's isolated references to Jesus as the Son of David (10:47–48; cf. also 12:35) into a major christological category that he employs not only descriptively, in relation to the person of Jesus, but also apologetically, against Israel. And whereas Mark makes no great use of the term *kyrios* ("Lord") as applied to Jesus (cf. 7:28; 10:51; 11:3), Matthew utilizes it numer-

ous times in order to underline his exalted station and divine author
ity. Along these same lines, Matthew also heightens the majesty of
Jesus' person by eliminating a number of Marcan references to his
"feelings," namely, that he was "angry" (Mark 3:5), was "moved
with pity" (Mark 1:41), "wondered" (Mark 6:6), "sighed deeply in
his spirit" (Mark 8:12), "became indignant" (Mark 10:14), or
looked upon a man and "loved" him (Mark 10:21). Finally,
Matthew also attributes to Jesus christological titles not found in
Mark, viz., "Emmanuel," "Servant," and "Son of Abraham."

Ecclesiologically, Mark gives the impression that, wherever his
place of writing, his community is free from the Jewish law and the
Pharisaic traditions surrounding it (cf. Mark 7:1–23). Matthew,
by contrast, writes in a situation in which Jewish and Jewish-Christian influence is most pronounced, as we shall see in chapter four.
Positively, he advocates the abiding validity of the law as Jesus has
interpreted it, and stresses in addition, on the part of the disciple, the
greater righteousness (5:17–20). Negatively, Matthew's community,
although suffering tribulation at the hands of gentiles (24:9; 10:22),
is experiencing even greater persecution at the hands of Jews (5:10–
12; 10:17, 23, 28; 23:34). Moreover, it is also beset internally by
severe moral and spiritual aberrations (24:10–12). In the face of
such problems, Matthew, with language that is often reminiscent of
Jewish apocalyptic, exhorts his fellow Christians on a broader scale
than Mark to single-hearted devotion to God (5:48) and loving
concern for the "brother" (chap. 18), threatening them with judgment and promising them eschatological reward (cf., e.g., 6:1, 4, 6,
18, 33; 13:49–50; 18:35).

As for the history of salvation, it is generally held that Mark was
written at about A.D. 70, close to the fall of Jerusalem. Matthew,
on the other hand, is removed from this event by a number of years.
In reflecting on the history of salvation, he tends to "periodize" more
than Mark. For one thing, he formally extends this history back-
wards to Abraham, and treats the "time of Israel (OT)" as a distinct
time of prophecy. By the same token, he introduces the so-called
formula quotations into his text and hence stresses in a special way
the "time of Jesus" as the time of eschatological fulfillment (cf., e.g.,
1:22–23; 2:15, 17–18; 4:14–16, etc.). Even the "time of Jesus"
is divided into discernible periods: the ministry of John (3:1–2), of

Jesus (4:17), of the disciples (10:5–7), and of the post-Easter church (24:14; 26:13), to the end of the age. By setting off the time of Jesus from the time of Israel (OT) and by dividing the time of Jesus into segments, Matthew is able to call attention in remarkably clear fashion to the time of Jesus as the age of salvation, to the person of Jesus as the basis of salvation, and to the post-Easter task of the church, the community of disciples of Jesus. In all of the above ways—christologically, ecclesiologically, and in terms of the history of salvation—Matthew shows that he found it necessary to revise Mark's Gospel.

If Matthew has revised Mark's Gospel, by what means has he done so? In all, the First Gospel comprises some 1068 verses. More than 600 of these, as we stated, can be traced to Mark, about 235 to Q, and the rest have come from oral or written traditions peculiar to Matthew himself. Now since Matthew has not for the most part composed freely but has taken over these traditions of the sayings of Jesus and of the narratives about him, it is obvious that he did not enjoy unrestricted freedom in composing a document that would "speak" to the church of his day. To write of the past in a way that would meet the needs of the present, Matthew made use of a number of literary devices that enabled him to interpret traditional materials by carefully editing them. What are some of these literary devices?

To begin with, Matthew arranges his sources in such a way as to *expand* upon the outline of Mark. Such expansion can be found at the beginning and end of the Gospel, within the body of the Gospel, and even within individual pericopes. To the story of John the Baptist, for instance, Matthew affixes a genealogy (1:2–17) and a cycle of infancy narratives (1:18–2:23). Whereas Mark has one resurrection narrative, Matthew has four (28:1–8, 9–10, 11–15, 16–20). Within the Gospel, the great speeches of Jesus represent in large measure Q and special material which Matthew has gathered together to form huge blocks of sayings or parables and fitted into the Marcan outline at prescribed points (cf. chaps. 5–7; 10; 11; 13; 18; 23; 24–25). The formula quotations of the OT provide examples of how Matthew can introduce material into single pericopes (cf., e.g., 21:1–9 [4–5] with Mark 11:1–10).

Some few additions in the Gospel appear to have been composed by Matthew himself. It may be that he was drawing upon older traditions which he either completely rewrote or first committed to writing. In any event, a minute analysis of the style, vocabulary, and contents of the pericopes on the origin of Jesus (1:18–25), Jesus' discussion with John (3:14–15), and the great commission (28:16–20), to cite but these, make it almost certain that these stem from the hand of Matthew himself.

In the second place, Matthew *rearranges* his sources. We have already observed this with respect to Q: Matthew groups the sayings of Jesus in this source to form great speeches (cf. chaps. 5–7; 10; 11; 13; 18; 23; 24–25). As for Mark, Matthew follows him with considerable fidelity throughout the last half of the Gospel (13:53–28:8), but in the first half (cf. 3:1–13:52) establishes a different sequence of events both by expanding upon Mark's outline and by transposing several Marcan pericopes to a new position (cf., e.g., 8:1–4 Mark 1:40–45; 9:1–17 Mark 2:1–22; 12:1–21 /Mark 2:23–3:12; 10:2–5a//Mark 3:13–19a).

Again, Matthew *abridges* his sources. Perhaps the best example of this is the manner in which he redacts the miracle stories of Mark. Take the healings of Jairus' daughter and the woman with a hemorrhage. Mark's account covers twenty-three verses (5:21–43). Matthew's account requires but nine (9:18–26): while retaining the words of Jesus, Matthew has dropped a large amount of narrative. The result is that under the pen of Matthew the two stories have become highly compact scenes depicting in dramatic fashion the encounter between Jesus, in whom God's power inheres, and persons in desperate need.

Fourth, Matthew *clarifies* his sources. Often this has to do with matters of style, as when Matthew changes Mark's awkward expression "those who were about him with the twelve" (4:10) to "the disciples" (13:10). But at times it is more far-reaching than this. Consider again the story of the woman with a hemorrhage. As Mark tells it, the woman comes up behind Jesus in the crowd and touches his garment (5:27). The sudden release of healing power seems to occur of itself (cf. 5:29–31). Only after the miracle has already taken place does Jesus sanction it (5:34). In Matthew's version, all this has changed. As soon as the woman touches Jesus' garment, he is pictured as turning around and confronting her (9:22). Not until he has explicitly sanctioned the healing does it take place (9:22d).

By editing the story in this fashion, Matthew shows that he is concerned that the reader labor under no false illusions: Jesus is most assuredly in complete control of all events surrounding the miracle; nothing happens without his knowledge or consent.

Last, Matthew *omits* material from his sources or *substitutes* one piece of tradition for another. An example of omission can be seen in the fact that Matthew takes over the verses that both precede and follow Mark 3:20–21, but leaves them. The reason is not hard to find: the notion that the relatives of Jesus should think him "mad" does not comply with Matthew's exalted understanding of his person. An example of substitution can be found in chapter 13: Matthew appropriates the whole of Mark 4 with the single exception that we find the parable of the tares (13:24–30) where we should expect to find the parable of the seed growing secretly (Mark 4:26–29).

Consequently, Matthew receives traditional materials and interprets them by redacting them, through expansion, rearrangement, abridgment, clarification, omission, and substitution. The grand result is that he creates a new literary document which narrates the gospel-story afresh to meet the needs of the church to which he belongs. And because Matthew does present his church with a new version of the gospel-story, a consideration of the composition of the Gospel calls for comment yet on his use of characters, of settings, and of the summary-passage.

The characters of the Gospel tend to play fixed roles. Jesus, of course, is the protagonist, the "hero" of the story. Angels are supernatural beings whose presence signals, or alludes to, the immediate or future intervention of God in human affairs, often on behalf of Jesus (cf. chaps. 1–2; 28). Satan is likewise a supernatural being, the transcendent adversary of Jesus. The disciples, upright persons such as "Joseph" (cf. 1:19), and people who approach Jesus in faith for healing are the "allies" of Jesus. The Israelite crowds form the background for much of Jesus' activity in public, but they remain unbelieving and in the passion narrative join their leaders in condemning Jesus to death. The Israelite leaders of whatever designation are the inveterate opponents of Jesus. Now since in Matthew's day Jesus is the Exalted One whom his church confesses and worships, the reader of the Gospel is not invited to identify with him per se, but with the disciples and people who come to him in faith. In learning of Jesus, the reader learns of the basis of salvation. In experiencing with the disciples their moments both of "understanding" and of "little faith," the reader is taught either positively or by reverse example what it means to be a follower of Jesus in post-Easter times.

It would be too much to say that Matthew attributes special meaning to more than a handful of the settings in which Jesus is described as carrying out his ministry. But some of the settings do possess a significance beyond what is strictly literal. Thus, "Galilee" is the place where Jesus proffers salvation to the Jews (4:12, 23) and where his church following Easter begins its mission of salvation to the gentiles (28:16–20). "Capernaum" and "Nazareth," the two cities in which Jesus is at home in Galilee (2:23; 4:13), are symbols of the rejection of divine grace (11:23–24; 13:54–58). "Jerusalem" is the place where Jesus must die (16:21). It is the "home" of such as are his mortal enemies—Herod (chap. 2), Pilate (chap. 27), and the "chief priests and the elders of the people" (cf., e.g., 2:4; 21:23; 26:3, 47; 27:1). The "mountain," as we shall see, is the place that alludes to Jesus as the Son of God. The "temple," as the dwelling place of God, is depicted as superseded through death and resurrection by the person of the Son of God (26:61; 27:51). And the phrase "in those days" (3:1; chap. 24) connotes, as we shall learn, the "last times" that will culminate in Jesus' visible return in glory for judgment.

As for the summary-passage, Matthew deftly employs it in order to alert the reader to the direction the plot of the gospel-story will take. Two sets of three summary-passages each dominate the greater part of the Gospel. In 4:7–11:1, the passages are 4:23(–25); 9:35; and 11:1. They describe Jesus as discharging throughout the whole of Galilee a ministry of teaching, preaching, and healing among the people. In this section of the Gospel, Jesus is pictured as unstintingly offering himself to Israel in word and deed as its Messiah. But Israel rejects Jesus (chaps. 11-12). Because this rejection functions as the occasion for Matthew to effect the great turning point in the plot of the gospel-story (chap. 13), he informs the reader at once of the shape of things to come: "But the Pharisees went out and took counsel against him, how to destroy him" (12:14). This passage, in turn, prepares the reader for the three summary-passages that set the tone for the final third of the Gospel: the passion-predictions (16:21;

17:22–23; 20:17–19). In ever greater detail, these predictions repeatedly remind the reader that the ineluctable direction the gospel-story will take is, according to God's decree (16:21), towards the cross and resurrection.

Thus, the redaction-critical approach to Matthew's Gospel focuses above all on its composition. What kind of a document is it? What is its intention? How does the story develop? How have the sources been shaped? What type of church stands behind it? In what manner of historical situation was it written, and does it reflect this situation? What is peculiarly Matthaean about its portrait of Jesus and of the disciples? And what, in view of these queries, is its message? In the course of this book we hope to address these issues, beginning with a sketch of our own redaction-critical approach to the Gospel.

A Redaction-Critical Approach in Outline

The question we are still pursuing is that of the nature and purpose of Matthew's Gospel. Generally overlooked is the circumstance that Matthew himself suggests how they are to be defined. He does this with the expression he has coined "the gospel of the kingdom" (4:23; 9:35; 24:14; 26:13).

It should be observed that Matthew does not distinguish, as the present-day historian must, between the message *of* Jesus to Israel and the post-Easter message of the church *about* Jesus. Instead, he designates both as "the [this] gospel of the kingdom." In 4:23 and 9:35, for instance, Matthew describes Jesus Messiah, declared by God at his baptism to be his unique Son (cf. 3:17), as going around all Galilee proclaiming to Israel "the gospel of the kingdom." Similarly, in 24:14 and 26:13, he writes that what shall be proclaimed by the disciples, or church, of Jesus in all the inhabited world is "this gospel of the kingdom." Whether it is preached as a "testimony" to Israel or to the gentiles, this gospel, which may also be termed "the word of the kingdom" (13:19), effects for the hearer salvation or damnation (cf. 11:5c–6; 13:19, 23; 24:14).

Although Matthew utilizes this one expression to designate both the preaching of the earthly Jesus and of the post-Easter church, surprisingly he nowhere explains in a sentence what it means. How, then, is it to be understood? To ascertain this, we must consider briefly the constituent terms "gospel" and "kingdom."

The stem *euaggel-* is at the basis of the Greek words for "gospel" (*euaggelion*) and "to proclaim (announce) news" (*euaggelizomai*). Whether or not the earthly Jesus ever employed these or equivalent terms in connection with his proclamation of the message of the kingdom of God is difficult to know. For his part, however, Matthew was heir to Q and Mark. Q, it appears, arose in a Jewish-Christian community that sprang up in the first years following the resurrection and maintained itself in a Palestinian environment. In this community, the verb "to announce news" (cf. Matt. 11:5 Luke 7:22) referred in all likelihood to a preaching of the coming in the near future of Jesus Son of man.

Whereas Matthew found the verb "to announce news" in Q, he appropriated the noun "gospel" from Mark. In Mark, this word is indissolubly joined to the person of Jesus as the Messiah. The emphasis is not solely on his return as the Son of man (cf. Mark 8:38; 9:1; 13:24–27; 14:62), but also on his ministry, death, and resurrection. Indeed, "gospel" in Mark is definite and most often absolute in character ("the gospel," 1:15; 8:35; 10:29; 13:10; 14:9), and denotes the proclamation of God's decisive act of salvation on behalf of humankind in Jesus Messiah, above all in his death and resurrection (cf., e.g., 1:1, 14–15; 8:29; 14:61; 15:32, 39; 16:6).

Matthew, then, brings together in his Gospel the Q tradition, which contains the verb *euaggelizomai* (meaning "to announce the imminent coming of Jesus Son of man"), and the Marcan tradition, which highlights the noun *to euaggelion* (meaning "the gospel [Jesus Christ]"). Since he employs the verb only once (cf. the Q logion 11:5) but works editorially with the noun (4:23; 9:35; 24:14; 26:13), we may conclude that it is the latter that is of special interest to him.

Now the expression "the [this] gospel of the kingdom" in Matthaean thought is thoroughly christological in coloration. It may not seem so at first glance, because it reads "the gospel *of the kingdom*." Still, in 4:23 and 9:35, it refers to the message that specifically Jesus Messiah, the Son of God, proclaims. And in 26:13, "this gospel," which denotes the message the disciples are to proclaim throughout the whole world, includes also mention of the woman's act of pouring oil on the head of Jesus (cf. 26:6–13). In other words, in these three passages we have solid evidence that in the church of Matthew the term "gospel" encompassed at once traditions of sayings of Jesus and traditions of narratives about him. In view of this, we may define the term "gospel" in the expression "the gospel of the kingdom" as the news about the kingdom, which saves or condemns, that is revealed in and through Jesus Messiah, the Son of God, and is announced first to Israel and then to the gentiles.

What is the meaning of the term "kingdom"? To begin with, the absolute designation "the kingdom" is simply an abbreviation of the fuller idiom "the kingdom of heaven." Although statistics reveal that Matthew prefers the latter to "the kingdom of God," the two expressions are synonymous. Because the genitive "(of) heaven" is subjective in nuance and a metonym for "God," the purpose of the expression "the kingdom of heaven" is to assert the truth that "God rules (reigns)." Hence, "the rule of God," or "the reign of God," is a proper paraphrase of it.

The notation in 4:23 and 9:35 that Jesus goes about Galilee proclaiming the gospel of the kingdom calls to mind the passages 3:2; 4:17; and 10:7, where Matthew pictures John the Baptist, Jesus, and the disciples as all announcing that "the kingdom of heaven is at hand (ēggiken)." The Greek verb ēggiken in these summary statements denotes a "coming near," an "approaching," that is spatial or temporal in character. In the light of this, it becomes evident that what Matthew depicts John, Jesus, and the twelve as proclaiming to Israel is that the rule of God has drawn near. Thus, we recognize that if the term "gospel" in the Matthaean expression "the gospel of the kingdom" finds its center in the person of Jesus Messiah, the Son of God, the term "kingdom" finds its center in the person of God. At the same time, even the term "kingdom" in the First Gospel is not without a christological focus, for Matthew states in words of the OT in 1:23 that it is in the son born to the virgin that God draws near to dwell with his people. In line with these emphases, therefore, the entire expression "the gospel of the kingdom" may be delineated as follows: it is the news which saves or condemns, that is revealed in and through Jesus Messiah, the Son of God, and is proclaimed first to Israel and then to the gentiles to the effect that in him the eschatological rule of God has drawn near to humankind.

Working with this definition, we can at last attempt to define the nature and the purpose of the First Gospel. We mentioned above that Matthew nowhere explicitly informs the reader how he is to understand the expression "the gospel of the kingdom." Instead, he simply assumes that when he uses it, the reader or hearer will know what is meant. On what grounds is he able to make this assumption? He can do so on the grounds that the reader or hearer has access to the document he has written. Accordingly, although Matthew does not employ the expression "the gospel of the kingdom" to denote a written document per se, in the final analysis it is the contents of his document—the words of Jesus and the narratives about him—that elucidate this expression. In recognition of this, there is consequently justification for arguing that the document Matthew has written is in fact of the nature of a "gospel." As we have seen, it sets forth news revealed in and through Jesus Messiah, the Son of God, and so may be termed a "kerygmatic portrait of history." Hence, we conclude that Matthew's document is of the nature of a "gospel," that is to say, a kerygmatic portrait of history. Its purpose is, again, to announce the news, which saves or condemns, that is revealed in and through Jesus Messiah, the Son of God, and is proclaimed first to Israel and then to the gentiles to the effect that in him the eschatological rule of God has drawn near to humankind.

A look at the two chief structural features of the Gospel corroborates this understanding of its nature and purpose. The first is the topical outline that governs the arrangement of the contents. At 4:17 and 16:21, Matthew brings the following formula: "From that time on Jesus [Christ] began. . . ." As is obvious, this formula signals the beginning of a new phase in the life and ministry of Jesus. In addition, each of the verses in which the formula is embedded stands apart to a degree from its context and sounds the theme that Matthew subsequently develops throughout a larger portion of his Gospel. Hence, if we construe these verses, and 1:1 as well, as "superscriptions" and press them thematically, this topical outline readily emerges: (I) The Person of Jesus Messiah (1:1–4:16); (II) The Public Proclamation of Jesus Messiah (4:17–16:20); and (III) The Suffering, Death, and Resurrection of Jesus Messiah (16:21–28:20).

We remarked in our discussion of the historical-biographical approach to the First Gospel that some commentators translate the opening words of 1:1 as "The book of the history of Jesus Messiah . . ." and maintain that they serve as the title of the entire Gospel.

The Greek word they translate as "history" in 1:1 is *geneseōs*. It occurs again in the nominative case in 1:18 (*genesis*). Since Matthew has formulated v. 18 so that it might refer back to v. 1 by way of v. 17 ("Messiah") and v. 16 ("from whom *was born Jesus* who is called the *Messiah*"), he shows that the word *genesis* must be translated the same way in both places. In v. 18, the meaning of this word is "origin." Necessarily, then, the proper translation of the opening words of v. 1 is "The book of the origin of Jesus Messiah. . . ." Concerning this translation, in Gen. 5:1 of the LXX (cf. also Gen. 2:4a) the words "the book of the origin" introduce a section that contains both a genealogy and related narrative material (cf. Gen. 5:1–6:8). In Matt. 1:1, these words do the same thing. This strongly suggests, therefore, that Matt. 1:1 is not to be thought of as the title of the whole of the Gospel but of the first main part (1:1–4:16). This part begins with a genealogy (1:1–17) and continues with other narratives (1:18–4:16) all of which contribute directly to Matthew's description of the person of Jesus Messiah.

But how, specifically, does Matthew's topical outline undergird what we have said of the nature and purpose of the Gospel? In speaking of the nature and purpose of the Gospel, we stated that it is a kerygmatic portrait of history that sets forth news that is revealed in and through Jesus Messiah, the Son of God. The topical outline confirms the truth of this statement both by indicating how the term "kerygmatic portrait of history" is to be understood and by culminating in each of its three main parts in a scene that portrays Jesus precisely as the Messiah, the Son of God.

As for the term "kerygmatic portrait of history," Matthew's Gospel assumes, of course, the contours of a "life of Jesus." This "portrait" is "kerygmatic," not in the narrow sense that Matthew intends it simply to serve the task of his church's preaching, but in the broader sense that it tells this community of the person of Jesus (cf. 1:1, 22–23; 2:15; 3:17; 4:3, 6), of his ministry of teaching, preaching, and healing (cf. 4:23; 9:35; 11:1), and of his suffering, death, and resurrection (cf. 16:21; 17:22–23; 20:17–19).

As for the scenes in which the three main parts of the Gospel culminate, the central pericopes in 1:1–4:16 are the stories of the origin of Jesus (1:18–25) and of the baptism (3:13–17). In the story of the origin of Jesus, Matthew writes in words of Isaiah that the son born to the virgin will be "Emmanuel," that is to say, the Son of God, for in his person "God is with us" (1:23). And in the story of the baptism, Matthew depicts God himself as openly declaring in the presence of John that Jesus is in fact his unique Son (3:16–17).

To turn to the second and third main parts of the Gospel (4:17–16:20; 16:21–28:20), one climactic pericope is the story of Peter's confession (16:13–20). Here Matthew pictures Peter at Caesarea Philippi as confessing in the company of the disciples, by revelation of God, that Jesus is none other than the Messiah, the Son of God (16:16–17). And at the end of the Gospel, the culminating pericope is that of the Great Commission (28:16–20). In this narrative, the exalted Jesus, to whom God has entrusted all authority in heaven and on earth, refers to himself as "the Son" (28:19), thus revealing that he stands before his disciples and commissions them exactly in his capacity as the resurrected Messiah, the Son of God.

Consequently, all three main parts of Matthew's topical outline stress in a special way his Son-of-God Christology. On the whole, this topical outline substantiates what we said of the nature and purpose of the Gospel by singling out the person of Jesus Son of God, especially his activity in public and his death and resurrection, as the "place" where God encounters people with his eschatological rule.

The second chief structural feature of the Gospel that corroborates our understanding of its nature and purpose is Matthew's concept of the history of salvation. The so-called formula quotations (1:22–23; 2:6, 15, 17–18, 23; 4:14–16; 8:17; 12:17–21; 13:14–15, 35; 21:4–5; 27:9–10), which owe their presence in the text to Matthaean redaction, indicate in broad lines how this concept is to be defined. In these unique passages, a quotation of the OT is introduced by words that emphasize its "fulfillment" in some phase of the life of Jesus. Structurally, therefore, these passages show that Matthew makes a basic distinction between the "time of Israel (OT)" as the time of prophecy and the "time of Jesus" as the time of fulfillment. Because Matthew traces the genealogy of Jesus back to Abraham (1:1, 17), it is plain that he conceives of the "time of Israel (OT)" as having begun with him.

Matthew employs the phrase "[in] those days" to make this same distinction. In chapter 24, this phrase denotes the "last times" that precede the parousia of Jesus Son of man and the consummation of the age (vv. 3, 19, 22, 29). By using it also at 3:1, Matthew explains that these "last times" burst upon Israel when John the Baptist appeared in the desert of Judea and summoned the people to repentance in preparation of the coming of their Messiah (3:1–12). Still, Matthew likewise asserts through his quotation of Isaiah in 1:23 that it is at the birth of the virgin's son that he will be called "Emmanuel," for it is from that moment on that "God is with us." In other words, according to Matthew the "last times" that will lead up to the end of all things began with the birth of Jesus but did not break publicly upon the scene of history until John the Baptist "in those days" embarked upon his ministry. Nevertheless, the distinction is the same: the "last times" that extend from the birth of Jesus to his parousia, that is to say, the "time of Jesus (earthly—exalted)," are to be distinguished from previous times, that is to say, the "time of Israel (OT)."

Consequently, Matthew differentiates fundamentally between two epochs: the "time of Jesus (earthly—exalted)" and the "time of Israel (OT)." Within the overarching time of Jesus, however, he also develops, we know, a sequence of temporal subcategories: there is the ministry to Israel of John (3:1–2), of Jesus (4:17, 23; 9:35; 15:24), and of the disciples (10:5–7), and the ministry to the gentiles of the post-Easter church (24:14; 26:13; 28:19–20). Because Matthew "periodizes" in this manner, it should be observed that he does not operate with a "time of the church" that stands apart from the time of Jesus. In Matthew's concept of the history of salvation, the so-called time of the church, Matthew's own time, is characterized by the ministry to the gentiles which the post-Easter disciples carry out in the final period of the time of Jesus under the guidance of the exalted Son of God.

If this is the way in which Matthew characterizes his own age of the church, how does he characterize the whole of the "time of Jesus (earthly—exalted)"? We discover this in the passages 1:23 and 28:20, which form a bracket around the Gospel and hence constitute what is known as an "inclusion." In these verses, and in 18:20 as well, Matthew informs us that the mark of the time of Jesus is the fact that in the person of Jesus Messiah, his Son, God has drawn near to dwell with his people, the church, thus inaugurating the eschatological age of salvation which is moving towards the consummation.

Now in defining the nature and purpose of the First Gospel, we described it as being kerygmatic and as setting forth the news, which saves or condemns, that is proclaimed first to Israel and then to the gentiles. In his concept of the history of salvation, Matthew points within the "time of Jesus (earthly—exalted)" to the ministry to Israel of John (3:1–2), of the earthly Jesus (4:17, 23; 9:35; 15:24), and of the disciples (10:5–7), and to the ministry to the gentiles of the post-Easter church (24:14; 26:13; 28:19–20). According to Matthew, therefore, Israel has been decisively confronted with the news that saves or condemns, and this news is furthermore being proclaimed to the gentiles. In short, Matthew's concept of the history of salvation substantiates what we said of the nature and purpose of the Gospel in that it reveals that God's activity in his Son is of ultimate significance for Israel and the gentiles alike.

Thus far, we have defined the nature and purpose of the First Gospel and discussed its two chief structural features, the topical outline and the concept of the history of salvation. One thing yet remains: to specify the central thought that governs the Gospel.

We have made repeated references in the last paragraphs to the passages 1:23 and 28:20 (cf. also 18:20), which "enclose" the Gospel. These passages express the thought that *in the person of Jesus Messiah, his Son, God has come to dwell to the end of time with his people, the church, thus inaugurating the eschatological age of salvation.* If we consider this thought carefully, we will recognize that it contains *in nuce* everything we have said until now about the nature and purpose of the Gospel and about its topical outline and concept of salvation-history. This thought is the one that controls Matthew's Gospel.

Of great importance is the fact that in this central thought the theology, Christology, and ecclesiology of Matthew can be seen to converge. On the one hand, the notion that "God is present with his eschatological rule in the person of Jesus" describes the relationship Matthew establishes between theology and Christology, between God the Father and his Son Jesus (cf. also 11:25–27; 28:18). On the other hand, the notion that "God in the person of Jesus is with us" is Matthew's own description of the relationship he establishes between Christology and ecclesiology, between Christ and his church (cf. 1:23; 28:20; also 18:20). The factor that ties these statements together is of course "Jesus," which means that Matthew's Gospel is essentially christological in orientation: it is only by attending to Jesus Messiah, the Son of God, that we shall come to know who God is and what the church is.

In view of all this, our further task in this book is now clear, viz., to treat in terms of the central thought of the Gospel Matthew's understanding of Christ (chapter two), of God (chapter three), and of the church (chapter four). As the concluding portion of chapter four, we shall also treat of the situation of Matthew.

MATTHEW'S UNDERSTANDING
OF CHRIST

We have discovered that the central thought of the First Gospel is that in the person of Jesus Messiah, his Son, God has drawn near to dwell to the end of time with his people, the church, thus inaugurating the eschatological age of salvation (cf. 1:23; 18:20; 28:20). In this chapter and the next, we want to explore the ramifications of particularly the first part of this central thought, viz., that it is in the person of Jesus Messiah, his Son, that God is present among humankind. In line with this, our concern in this chapter is with the Christology of the First Gospel, and our goal is to trace Matthew's portrait of Jesus. Since the topical outline of the Gospel shows that Matthew has organized his materials to focus, in turn, on the person of Jesus Messiah (1:1–4:16) and on his public ministry (4:17–16:20) and death and resurrection (16:21–28:20), we shall look to it to find the key to Matthew's portrait of Jesus.

The opinion is sometimes expressed that the best way to proceed in treating the Christology of the evangelists or of Paul is to strive to capture the overall picture each one sketches in place of analyzing individual titles such as "Messiah," "Son of God," "Son of man," "Kyrios," etc. In the case of Matthew, however, the latter approach commends itself, on two counts: the various titles function in recognizable ways, and the relationships among them have been carefully drawn. Then, too, the precision and sophistication Matthew displays in working with christological titles should dispel at last the erroneous notion that his Christology is primitive and underdeveloped.[20] The truth of the matter is that Matthew has reflected in depth on the person of Jesus and has fashioned a sharply etched profile of him.

The term for Christ which Matthew uses more often than any other is "Jesus" (*Iēsous*). To facilitate the later discussion, we should observe here at the outset that it has in the First Gospel the status of a personal name. This is evident from the related circumstances that Matthew lists the son born to Mary in his genealogical table as "Jesus" (1:16) and also has Joseph, upon divine command, legally give him this name (1:21, 25).

Another indication that Matthew regards "Jesus" as a personal name is the fact that although the Gospel is not, as we learned, rich in biographical detail, what little can be found seems to be clustered around this word. Thus, the one Matthew calls "Jesus" is described as born in "Bethlehem" (2:1, 5–6) and raised in "Nazareth" (2:23; 21:11; 26:71). He is the "son of the carpenter," whose mother's name is, again, "Mary" (13:55). He has both "sisters" and "brothers," the names of the latter being "James," "Joseph," "Simon," and "Judas" (13:55–56). As an adult, he moves from Nazareth to "Capernaum" (4:13), which is known as "his own city" (9:1), where he apparently has a "house" (9:10, 28; 13:1, 36; 17:25). In Jerusalem to the south, he can be recognized, as can also his disciples, as one who comes "from Galilee" (cf. 26:69, 73; also 21:11).

On the other hand, there is one passage in which the term "Jesus" occurs which stands apart from the others: 1:21. Because "Jesus" means in essence "savior" ("Jahweh is salvation") and Matthew in 1:21 plays on this meaning ("You shall call his name 'Jesus,' for he shall *save* his people from their sins"), it looks as though "Jesus" in this passage ceases to be a mere personal name and attains the rank of a christological title. We shall see below, however, that it is not as "Jesus" per se that Matthew depicts the son of Mary as accomplishing salvation from sins, but as the "Son of God" (cf. 26:28 and 27:38–54). Hence, the reason Matthew plays on the word "Jesus" in 1:21 is to set forth the mission of the son born to Mary. On the whole, the character of the word "Jesus" as a personal name in the First Gospel is unmistakable.

Jesus as Messiah

The term "Messiah," or "Christ" (*christos*), is one of the first christological titles the earliest church ever applied to Jesus (cf. Acts 2:36). It was not long before it also became a personal name, often used in association with "Jesus" ("Jesus Christ"; cf., e.g., Rom. 1:1; 5:6, 8). For his part, Matthew utilizes the term in both ways.

Thus, in 1:1, 18; and 16:21, "Jesus Christ" is plainly a name, although in 1:18 the correct reading of the text is probably "Christ" and in 16:21 "Jesus." Even as a personal name, however, "Jesus Christ" conveys for Matthew the underlying truth that Jesus, born of Mary, is the Messiah, God's anointed (cf. 1:1, 18 to 1:16; 16:21 to 16:20).

While it is the High Priest and especially kings in the OT who are said to be the anointed of God (cf., e.g., Lev. 4:3; 6:22; 1 Sam. 12:3; 16:13; Lam. 4:20), prophets, too, could be so designated (Ps. 105:15; 1 Chron. 16:22). Since in three places in the First Gospel Jesus is called "prophet" (prophētēs), the question is whether Matthew views it as a predication of majesty.

The answer is unequivocally negative. For Matthew, "prophet" is the term that properly applies to OT figures such as Isaiah (cf., e.g., 3:3) or Jeremiah (cf., e.g., 2:17), or even to a circle of Christians within his own church (cf. 10:41; 23:34). But this is the extent of it. In relation to John the Baptist and Jesus, it is inappropriate because it connotes too little. Thus, the unbelieving Israelite "crowds" think of John as a prophet (14:5; 21:26). But Jesus declares to them that he is "more than a prophet" (11:7, 9); he is, in reality, the forerunner of the Messiah (11:10). These same "crowds," or "men," view Jesus as a prophet (16:13–14; 21:11, 46). But again, this is too little: such a "confession" implies no personal commitment to Jesus but only contrasts the populace with their leaders; these cannot even look upon Jesus as a prophet because they hold him to be an enemy they must destroy (21:46). Consequently, the true perception of the person of Jesus from Matthew's standpoint is not that he be regarded as a prophet but, as Peter confesses on behalf of the disciples, as the Messiah, the Son of God (cf. 16:14 with 16:16). If this is clear, we see that Jesus' statement in Nazareth that "a prophet is not without honor except in his own country and in his own house" (13:57) must be interpreted along the following lines: his former neighbors, like his worst enemies and unlike even the crowds, will not afford him so much as the honor due a prophet.

Accordingly, the term "prophet" is not a christological title in the First Gospel, and Matthew does not cast Jesus in the role of "Prophet-Messiah." How, then, does he understand the title "Messiah"?

In Matthew's scheme of things, the Messiah, that is, the Coming One foretold by the prophets and awaited by Israel (11:2–6), is a kingly figure. He is, to be sure, Jesus (1:16; 16:20; 24:5), who stands in the royal line of David (1:1, 16, 17, 20, 25) and brings the history of Israel to its culmination (1:1, 17). Invested with the authority of God, he means salvation or damnation for people (1:21; 3:11; 11:3, 6).

This is Matthew's initial description of Jesus as the Messiah. Throughout his Gospel he develops it further, in terms of two other christological designations. The first of these is the "King of the Jews (Israel)" (*basileus tōn Ioudaiōn [Israēl]*).

When Matthew relates the title "Messiah" to the "King of the Jews (Israel)," it assumes, from the vantage point of the characters in the gospel-story, political overtones that are uniformly negative. Herod, for instance, because he fears the loss of his throne, plots to kill the Messiah, the King of the Jews (2:2, 4, 13, 16). Pilate and the Roman cohort, in turn, accede to the charge that "Jesus . . . the King of the Jews . . . who is called the Messiah" is a political throne-pretender (27:11, 17, 22, 29, 37). In that the leaders of the people mock the crucified Messiah as the "King of Israel," they are pictured as taking up where the Romans have left off: Jesus, placed by the Romans on the cross as the "King of the Jews" (27:37), does not even have at his command sufficient power to get himself down and so prove this messianic "claim" for which he is being executed (cf. 26:63, 68 and 27:41–42).

The preceding are examples of what we may designate as the "public" concept of Jesus as the Messiah: such figures in the gospel-story as Herod and Pilate attempt to deal with Jesus the Messiah as though he were claiming for himself politically the throne of Israel. In stark contrast to this is Matthew's positive, or "confessional," description of Jesus as the Messiah. According to it, Jesus Messiah is depicted as the King who suffers on behalf of his people. By defining the kingship of Jesus Messiah in this way, Matthew effectively disabuses the reader of the Gospel of any notion that Jesus was the insurrectionist his enemies made him out to be.

To illustrate this, when Jesus enters Jerusalem as the Son of David (21:1–11), Matthew inserts into his Marcan text (cf. 11:1–10) a formula quotation that refers to him as the "humble King" (21:5).

This reference points ahead to chapter 27, which tells of the suffering Jesus endures as King at the hands of Pilate (vv. 11–31) and on the cross (vv. 38, 42). In the pericope 27:27–31, Matthew provides a detailed sketch of the true nature of Jesus' kingship: as he stands draped in a scarlet robe with a crown of thorns on his head and a reed for a scepter in his right hand, the soldiers abuse him and, kneeling in mock obeisance before him, hail him as "King of the Jews." Hence, it "King" marks Jesus Messiah as a political throne-pretender in the eyes of his enemies, in the eyes of Matthew it marks him as the one in the line of David (1:6, 20, 25; 21:9) who establishes his rule, not by bringing his people to heel, but by suffering on their behalf.

In Matthew's perspective, therefore, Jesus as the Messiah is not a prophetic but a royal figure. From the house of David, the entire history of Israel culminates in him, and he means salvation or damnation for people. As the "King of the Jews (Israel)," the "public" view of his person is that he is a political throne-pretender. In reality, however, he is the King of his people in the sense that he suffers on their behalf.

We stated earlier that Matthew develops the title "Messiah" in terms of two christological designations. If the one is the "King of the Jews (Israel)," the second one is the "Son of God." Furthermore, a glance at chapter 27 shows that in the story of Jesus on the cross (vv. 38–54), where the suffering of Jesus on behalf of others reaches its climax, the title "King of Israel" gives way to the title "Son of God" (cf. 27:40, 43, 54). What this means, as we shall discover shortly, is that Matthew's concept of Jesus as Messiah–King is taken up into his more expansive concept of Jesus as the Son of God. It is this title that names the category that is at the heart of Matthew's christology.

Jesus Messiah, the Son of God

We observed above that Matthew devotes the first main part of his topical outline to the person of Jesus Messiah (1:1–4:16). By so doing, he neatly points the way to his basic understanding of Jesus. To ascertain this, we shall consider briefly this first main part according to structure and content.

Because the First Gospel opens with a genealogy and infancy

narratives, which are followed in chapter 3 by the story of the public ministry of John the Baptist, the prevailing opinion among commentators is that chapters 1–2 stand apart from the rest of the Gospel and should be regarded as its prologue. Still, a careful study of 1:1–4:16 demonstrates that it must be construed as the first larger section of the Gospel.

Structurally, one indication of this is the presence in the Greek text at 3:1 of the particle *de* ("now," "then"). The context reveals that Matthew frequently utilizes this particle in the opening line of a story in order to connect that story with preceding narrative (cf., e.g., 1:18; 2:1, 13, 19; 4:12). By employing *de* at 3:1, Matthew shows that the interpreter is not to posit a fundamental break in the text between chapter 2 and chapter 3 but, on the contrary, is to view the pericopes of the two chapters as belonging together.

A second structural indication that the pericopes comprising chapters 1–2 and 3:1–4:16 are to be thought of as one larger section is the formula quotations in 2:23 and 4:12–16. It is generally held that the travels of Jesus prior to his public ministry come to an end when Joseph brings Mary and the infant Jesus from Egypt and settles in Nazareth (2:23). But a look at these formula quotations proves that these travels of Jesus do not in reality end until he takes up residence in Capernaum. It is to make this point that Matthew shapes the passage 4:12–14 in such a way that it takes up flawlessly on the earlier passage 2:22–23. These passages read as follows: ". . . he [Joseph, with Mary and the infant Jesus] *went and dwelt in a city called Nazareth*, that what was spoken by the prophets might be fulfilled . . ."; ". . . he [Jesus] *left Nazareth and went and dwelt in Capernaum* by the sea, in the regions of Zebulun and Naphtali, that what was spoken by the prophet Isaiah might be fulfilled. . . ."

This mention of the travels of Jesus prior to his public ministry calls attention to yet a third indication of the unity of 1:1–4:16, viz., all of the pericopes in this larger section narrate events that are *preliminary* to Jesus' ministry to Israel. When Jesus does finally appear openly in Israel, Matthew marks this with a massive summary-passage (4:23–25; cf. 4:17). But earlier, Jesus is pictured as leading a "private" existence, and there are only signs that he is about to undertake a public mission. When John, for example, carries out his ministry to Israel (3:1–12), Jesus is not present, so that John fore tells his coming (cf. 3:11–12). When John baptizes Jesus, he is the sole witness of this, for no reference is made to the crowds or to the Israelite leaders (cf. 3:5–7), and the force of the adverb "then" (*tote*) at 3:13 is that it removes chronologically and temporally the baptism of Jesus from previous events (cf. "then" also at 4:1).

All of the narratives that make up 1:1–4:16, therefore, have this "preliminary quality" about them. In addition, all of them can likewise be shown to stand in the service of one major theme. This is a fourth indication of the unity of 1:1–4:16. What this theme is comes to the fore in the series of related idioms with which Matthew punctuates the entire section: "his people" (1:21), "my people" (2:6), "my Son" (2:15; 3:17), and "the Son of God" (4:3, 6). In other words, the theme of the divine Sonship of Jesus Messiah permeates 1:1–4:16, so that both structurally and materially it reveals itself to be, again, the first main part of the Gospel.

To delineate Matthew's basic understanding of Jesus, we turn now to an investigation in context of the related idioms just cited. In the opening verse of the Gospel, Matthew describes Jesus Messiah as the "Son of David" and the "Son of Abraham." He is the Son of David because Joseph son of David, on divine command, gives him his name, adopting him into his line (1:20, 25). He is the Son of Abraham because the entire history of Israel, which bears promise also for the gentiles, reaches its culmination in him (1:17; 8:11). But though it is not said in 1:1, he is first of all the "Son of God" (*huios tou theou*).

As early as 1:16, Matthew seems to allude to the divine Sonship of Jesus Messiah. He casts the verb *gennaō* in the passive voice, in this way alerting the reader to special activity on the part of God ("Jesus *was born* [by an act of God]"). This verb, in turn, points forward, to the passive participle *gennēthen* ("that which *is conceived*") in 1:20, which also alludes to divine activity. This participle is found in the story on the origin of Jesus (1:18–25). In it, Matthew states less cryptically that Mary's conception was "by the Holy Spirit" (1:18, 20), that God through the prophet disclosed the true significance of the person of her son ("God with us," 1:22–23), that Mary was a "virgin" when she bore him (1:23), and that the child could not have been from Joseph because Joseph made no attempt to have relations with Mary until after she had given birth to her son (1:25).

When they are taken together, the intention of these terms and statements is clear: Matthew asserts that Jesus Messiah, born of Mary, is nevertheless the Son of God, for his origin is in God.

Chapter 1, especially vv. 18–25, is crucial to a proper grasp of the Christology of Matthew. Jesus Messiah is called the Son of Abraham, and as such he is the hope of the gentiles. He is also called the Son of David, and as such he is the hope of Israel. Yet it is as "Emmanuel," that is to say, as the Son of God, that he is "God with us," the one in whom God actually dwells with his people of both Jewish and gentile origin. Hence, what Matthew does in chapter 1 is to ascribe the fulfillment of messianic expectation associated with Abraham and David to Jesus as the Son of God.

This same phenomenon is in evidence elsewhere in the Gospel. Thus, although technically Jesus as the Son of Abraham is indeed the hope of the gentiles, it is Jesus as the exalted Son of God who finally commissions his followers to make disciples of all the nations (28:19–20). The title Son of God in the First Gospel envelopes the title Son of Abraham and supersedes it.

Since Jesus does not rise from the dead as Son of David, which means that this title in the First Gospel is applicable only to the earthly Jesus, it is apparent that beyond Easter the title Son of God likewise supersedes the title Son of David. Even this side of Easter, however, Matthew makes the title Son of God superior to the title Son of David. Adoption by Joseph son of David, for example, cannot compare to conception by the Holy Spirit (cf. 1:20, 25 with 1:18, 20). Furthermore, in several places in the Gospel OT Scripture relating to the house of David is recorded as attaining its fulfillment in Jesus as portrayed as the Son of God (cf. 1:23; 2:6; 3:17; 4:15–16; 17:5). The pericope on the question about David's son (22:41–46) also underlines the superiority of the divine Sonship of Jesus Messiah over his Davidic sonship.

This is not to say that Matthew discounts the Abrahamic or Davidic sonship of Jesus Messiah. Jesus is to be sure the Son of Abraham and the Son of David. In him the history of Israel, begun in Abraham and bearing promise for the gentiles, does in fact reach its culmination, and he does in truth stand in the line of David, discharging, as we shall learn, a portion of his ministry under the sign of this name. But the point Matthew is concerned to make is that

Jesus Messiah is preeminently the Son of God; what is more, this title encompasses also that expectation surrounding more particularly Abraham and David.

In chapter 2, Matthew continues his presentation of the person of Jesus Messiah. The Magi arrive in Jerusalem and ask where the newborn "King of the Jews" is to be found (2:2). Herod responds by designating this king as the "Messiah" (2:4), the one whom he anticipates will lay claim to his throne, as is obvious from his secret desire "to destroy" Jesus (2:13). By means of a formula quotation that cites the words of God to king David, Matthew sets forth the correct understanding of the royal Messiah: in reality, he is the eschatological Shepherd of "my people" Israel (2:5b–6).

Now it is highly significant that, following 2:6, Matthew never once refers to Jesus in chapter 2 as "king" or "ruler," but instead refers to him consistently as "the child" and repeatedly employs the expression "the child and [with] his mother" (cf. 2:8–9, 11, 13–14, 20–21). The remarkable thing about this latter expression is that it is at once appropriate to the narrative and a means by which Matthew can speak of Jesus without giving the impression that he is the son of Joseph and hence solely the Son of David (1:20, 25). On the contrary, in that Matthew makes reference to Jesus and Mary exclusive of Joseph, he recalls the situation of chapter 1: the virgin Mary gives birth to a son who has been conceived apart from Joseph son of David by the Holy Spirit (1:18, 20, 23). Thus, it becomes plain that the purpose of the expression "the child and [with] his mother" is to remind the reader that the son of Mary is at the same time the Son of God. Consequently, the term "the child" in chapter 2 reveals itself to be a surrogate for "Son of God," and Matthew himself confirms this observation: at 2:15, which is a formula quotation, he breaks his otherwise consistent use throughout 2:7–23 of the expression "the child and [with] his mother" so that none other than God, through the prophet, might call "the child" Jesus "my Son." In the last analysis, therefore, we see that "the child" whom the Magi come to Bethlehem to "worship" (2:11) as the "King of the Jews" is in fact the "Son of God," just as "the child" whom Herod plots to kill is no political throne-pretender but the eschatological Shepherd of God's people who is likewise the "Son of God."

In the pericope on John the Baptist (3:1–12), Matthew depicts John as referring to Jesus as the "mightier One" whose coming is imminent and will result in salvation or damnation for Israel (vv. 11–12). This reference creates anticipation in the mind of the reader for the appearance of Jesus at his baptism.

The story of the baptism (3:13–17) contains several important emphases. For one thing, Jesus does not submit to baptism by John because he, like Israel, has need to repent of sin (cf. 3:2, 6, 11) or because he would become a disciple of John, but because it is God's will that he and John should "fulfill all righteousness" (3:15). Jesus' baptism, then, reflects the circumstance that he is perfectly obedient to his Father's will.

The occurrence of the words "and behold" at 3:16b and 3:17a indicates that it is in these verses, especially the latter, that the story of the baptism culminates. The purpose of the opening of the heavens is both to permit the Spirit to descend and to signal that divine revelation is about to take place (cf. Ezek 1:1). The descent of the Spirit upon Jesus denotes the divine act whereby God empowers him to discharge the messianic ministry he is shortly to begin (4:17). Such "empowerment," of course, is not to be interpreted as Jesus' initial endowment with the Spirit, for he was conceived by the Spirit; instead, it is a commentary on what it meant for John to designate him as the "mightier One" (3:11). The words of the voice from heaven, "This is my beloved Son, with whom I am well pleased" (3:17), declare Jesus, precisely in his capacity as the only, or unique, Son of God, to be the Messiah from the house of David whom God has chosen to bring his eschatological rule to humankind (cf. 1:23; 4:17, 23; 9:35; 12:28; 21:37; 24:14; 28:18b–20).

In the declaration of the heavenly voice at 3:17, we have reached the apex, not only of the story of the baptism, but also of the entire first main part of Matthew's Gospel (1:1–4:16). In this part, Matthew describes the person and origin of Jesus. The overriding truth he promulgates is that Jesus, who is the royal Messiah, is uniquely the Son of God. He does not state this truth in 1:1, the heading of the first main part of the Gospel, for, as something that can be known solely by revelation (16:16–17), it must first be proclaimed, not by any character in the gospel-story and not even by himself, the author, but only by God. Accordingly, Matthew alludes to this truth with circumlocutions (1:16, 18, 20), with metaphors (2:8–9, 11, 13–14, 20–21; 3:11), or with a term ("son") that is susceptible of dual meaning (1:21, 23, 25), and he even permits it to sound softly as the word of the Lord spoken through the prophet (1:22–23; 2:15). Still, all remains adumbration until that climactic point following the baptism of Jesus when the voice from heaven "publicly" proclaims in the presence of John that Jesus is indeed the unique Son of God.

The story of the temptation (4:1–11) flows from the climactic verse 3:17 even as the previous narratives have tended towards it. It develops in particular one aspect of the divine Sonship of Jesus, viz., his perfect obedience to the will of God. Three times Satan tempts Jesus in his capacity as the Son of God. In that these temptations are antitypical to those experienced by the Israelites in their wanderings from Egypt to Canaan, Jesus is portrayed as recapitulating in his person this history of Israel, who had also been designated by God as his son (Exod. 4:22–23). But whereas Israel son of God broke faith with God, Jesus Son of God renders to him perfect obedience.

The pericope 4:12–16 is transitional in nature. Its purpose is to place Jesus, whom Matthew has presented in full as Messiah Son of God, in Galilee, where he will begin his public ministry to Israel.

On the strength of the preceding discussion, we can now return to the series of related idioms we listed above—"his people" (1:21), "my people" (2:6), "my Son" (2:15; 3:17), and "the Son of God" (4:3, 6)—and draw together the contents of the passages in which they occur. In combination, these passages provide us with a summary sketch of the Christology of the first main part of Matthew's Gospel. This sketch is the following: Jesus, in the line of David (1:21), is the Son of God (2:15; 3:17), that is to say, he has his origin in God (1:20) and is the one chosen to shepherd the eschatological people of God (2:6), for, empowered by God for messianic ministry (3:16–17), he proves himself in confrontation with Satan to be perfectly obedient to the will of God (4:3–4, 5–7, 8–10); as such a one, he saves his (God's) people from their sins (1:21).

The Son of God as One Who Teaches, Preaches, and Heals

Matthew begins his Gospel by portraying Jesus Messiah above all as the Son of God, which means in a nutshell that in him God has drawn near with his eschatological rule to dwell with his people (1:23). The second and third main parts of the Gospel have to do with the public ministry of Jesus Messiah (4:17–16:20) and with his suffering, death, and resurrection (16:21–28:20). What kind of activity does the Messiah, the Son of God, undertake in Israel? What does he do among the people? To know this is to comprehend better Matthew's portrait of him.

Before we look at specific modes of the activity of Jesus, mention must be made of certain aspects of his divine Sonship not yet spelled out. From all we have said it should be obvious that, in Matthew's eyes, Jesus is the Son of God in a manner that cannot be predicated to any other human being. Through him the disciples, for example, enter into fellowship with God and hence become "sons of God" (4:18–22; 5:9, 45), but he alone is the "Son of God." For this reason, Jesus speaks of God in the First Gospel as "my Father" (cf., e.g., 10:32–33; 12:50; 16:17) or, with an eye to the disciples, as "your Father" (cf., e.g., 5:16, 45, 48), but never as "our Father." The Lord's Prayer is no exception to this, because "our Father" (6:9) are words the disciples as a group are to utter in their approach to God.

Since Jesus is uniquely the Son of God, the relationship he has with God is unique. This is implied already in his conception by the Holy Spirit (1:18, 20) and by his empowerment with the Spirit at baptism (3:16). But it is in the pericope on Jesus' thanksgiving to the Father (11:25–27) that this is most emphatically brought out. In this pericope Jesus Messiah, "the Son" (v. 27), both addresses God as "Father" (vv. 25–26) and employs the absolute expression "the Father" (v. 27). The unique relationship between the Son and the Father is characterized by the verb "to know" (*epignōskō*, v. 27). This verb connotes that there exists total unity of will between the Father and the Son, and what this means is that, on the one hand, the Father elects the Son and authorizes him to represent him in the world and, on the other, that the Son acknowledges this election by living in complete fellowship with the Father, rendering to him perfect obedience. In addition, because the Son and the Father "know" each other, it is the Son who alone "reveals" the Father to people (v. 27), through all he says and all he does, that is, through his messianic ministry (cf. 11:2–6).

In consequence of the unique relationship that exists between Jesus Messiah, the Son of God, and God his Father, the Father entrusts the Son with divine authority (*exousia*). The upshot is that what the

Son says and does is said and done on the authority of God; God himself is fully active in the messianic ministry of his Son.

Matthew never tires of making this point. Often he does so obliquely, but in select passages he does so explicitly. In the Sermon on the Mount, for example, it is as one invested with divine authority that the Matthaean Jesus declares: "You have heard that it was said to the men of old . . . but I say to you . . ." (5:21–22, 27–28, 31–32, 33–34, 38–39, 43–44). At the conclusion of this sermon, Matthew writes: "the crowds were astonished at his teaching, for he taught them as one who had authority . . ." (7:28–29). In 11:27, Jesus Messiah exclaims: "All things have been given over to me by my Father. . . ." In the pericope on the question about authority (21:23–27), the thrust of Jesus' argument is that just as John the Baptist carried out his ministry on the authority of God, so he, the Son of God, wields in the house of God through teaching (21:23) and healing (21:14) the authority of God. In 28:18, the exalted Son of God asserts: "All authority in heaven and on earth has been given to me." Finally, in one passage Jesus claims divine authority for himself, not as the Son of God, but as the Son of man (9:6). This ostensible anomaly we shall explain below.

Jesus Messiah, then, is the divine Son who speaks and acts on the authority of God his Father. In describing the messianic activity of Jesus in Israel, Matthew states that he "teaches," "preaches," and "heals" (4:23; 9:35; 11:1). What is the significance of these terms?

We begin with the verb "to preach" (kēryssō), since it is used less frequently than the others. If we ask whom Matthew reports as "preaching," it is first of all John the Baptist. John proclaims repentance in view of the nearness of the kingdom of heaven (3:1–2), and the focus of his proclamation is on Jesus, the "mightier One" whose coming means salvation or damnation for people (3:11–12). Next, Jesus himself is said to preach, and his proclamation, like that of John, announces repentance in view of the nearness of the kingdom of heaven (4:17; cf. also 4:23; 9:35; 11:1). The heart of his message, we learned, is that in his own person and work God's eschatological rule is a present reality. Third, the disciples of Jesus are likewise enjoined to preach, and they, too, announce the nearness of the kingdom (10:7). Their preaching is an extension of Jesus' ministry; hence, their message has the same content as his. Last, mention is also made that the church following Easter will preach (24:14; 26:13). Once again, the focus of this message is on the person and work of Jesus.

What this survey shows is that the function of the verb "to preach" in the First Gospel is to establish continuity of ministry and message among John, Jesus, the disciples, and the post-Easter church. In other words, Matthew utilizes this verb to inform the reader that throughout the entire "time of Jesus (earthly–exalted)," which extends from his birth to his parousia, and therefore throughout the successive ministries of John, of the earthly Jesus, of the disciples, and of the post-Easter church, the message of the kingdom, which finds its center in God's activity in Jesus Messiah, the Son of God, has been, is being, and will be, proclaimed. Accordingly, Matthew draws upon this verb to assert to the members of his church that Jesus preached the gospel of the kingdom (4:23; 9:35) and that they preach the gospel of the kingdom (24:14; 26:13). Matthew's purpose is to make them aware that "now," just as "then," it is the proclamation of this message that results in the salvation or damnation of people.

Because the verb "to preach" (*kēryssō*) in the First Gospel stresses continuity of ministry and message as regards John, Jesus, the disciples, and the church, it is not singularly indicative of the activity of Jesus. It would not be in keeping with Matthew's thinking, therefore, to describe Jesus as the "Preacher." Strictly speaking, he is not the "preacher" in a way others are not.

Of the three verbs with which Matthew describes the activity of the Messiah, the Son of God, in Israel, the verb "to teach" (*didaskō*) in 4:23; 9:35; and 11:1 has the position of stress. This indicates that Matthew attaches special importance to it. If Matthew would not call Jesus the "Preacher," would he call him the "Teacher"?

The answer is decidedly negative if this means that "teacher" is to be construed as a predication of majesty. In chapter one, we pointed out that Matthew, unlike Mark, never permits the disciples to address Jesus with the synonymous terms of "rabbi" or "teacher," but only the traitor Judas (26:25, 49) and such strangers or opponents as a "scribe" (8:19), "some of the scribes and Pharisees" (12:38), the rich "young man" (19:16, 22), the "disciples" of the Pharisees and the "Herodians" (22:16), the "Sadducees" (22:23–24), and a "lawyer" who tempts him (22:36). The disciples, by contrast, consistently address Jesus as "Lord." In only one place does Jesus instruct the disciples to refer to him as "teacher" (26:18), and this is in connection with a conversation they are to have with a stranger in which "teacher" expresses the way in which this man will regard Jesus (26:17–19). Thus, as far as Matthew is concerned, "rabbi" and "teacher" are terms of human respect. As the proverb 10:24 puts it, they denote the kind of respect a disciple owes his mentor or a slave his master.

Consequently, "teacher" in the First Gospel is not a christological title but a public term of human respect by which Matthew pictures strangers and opponents of Jesus as approaching him as though he were no more than one Jewish rabbi among others. But in what manner, then, does Matthew characterize Jesus in those scenes in which he pictures him as the one who delivers authoritative instruction to the disciples, or church? Matthew gives us the answer in 23:8–10: it is Jesus the "Messiah" who is the one teacher of the disciples. But on this view, how would Matthew have us understand his use here of the title "Messiah"? From previous discussion, from Peter's confession in 16:16, and from the question of the high priest in 26:63, it is clear that the one teacher of the disciples, or church, is Jesus Messiah, the Son of God. But should this be correct, why does Matthew not bring the title Son of God in 23:8–10?

This has to do with the nature of this title. In 16:17, Matthew says in a logion of Jesus that it is only by divine revelation that any human being can penetrate the mystery of his person and know him to be the Messiah, the Son of God. Those who utter the title Son of God apart from divine revelation do so in ignorance of its true meaning and hence make themselves guilty of blasphemy and mockery (cf. 26:63–66; 27:39–43). In Matthew's eyes, therefore, "Son of God" is not a "public" title, for Jesus is not recognized in public to be the Son of God. But in 23:1, Matthew records that it is in the company of the "crowds" as well as of the disciples that Jesus speaks the words of 23:8–10. The answer, therefore, is that Matthew does not bring the title Son of God in 23:8–10 because the very setting he has established precludes for him the use of it. In any event, the statement stands: the one teacher of the disciples, or church, is Jesus Messiah, the Son of God.

In setting forth the teaching activity of Jesus Messiah, the Son of God, Matthew emphasizes one factor in particular: he makes known the will of God in terms of its original intention. For Matthew, the Son of God is the mouthpiece of God in a direct and immediate fashion. In a variety of ways Matthew calls attention to this. For one thing, he remarks that Jesus teaches with an authority not found among the scribes, and depicts the crowds as being astonished by it (7:28–29). Indeed, Jesus teaches in a way that makes of him the supreme interpreter of the law; his word is more radical than that of Moses and can even stand above it (cf. 5:2, 17–18, 21–22, 27–28, 31–32, 33–34, 38–39, 43–44; 19:7–9). In disputes between Jesus and the Israelite leaders over matters of law, Matthew, in comparison, for instance, with Mark, prefers to stress the fact that Jesus speaks the mind not merely of Moses but, more importantly, of God.

The three examples of the latter are worthy of note. In debate with the "Pharisees and scribes" over the law and the tradition of the elders, Matthew does not, like Mark, have Jesus introduce his quotation of the law with the words "For *Moses* said . . ." (Mark 10:7), but with the words "For *God* said . . ." (15:4). Again, in debate with the "Pharisees" on divorce Matthew redacts Mark's pericope in order to emphasize more strongly than the latter the supersession of the will of Moses by the will of God (cf. 19:4b, 7–8 with Mark 10:3b–6). Last, in debate with the "Sadducees" over the question of the resurrection, Matthew emends Mark's version of the words of Jesus (". . . have you not read *in the book of Moses* . . . how *God* said to him . . ."; Mark 12:26) to read: ". . . have you not read what was said to you by *God* . . ." (22:31), thus eliminating a reference to Moses and making the reference to God stand out more starkly.

That Jesus Messiah, the Son of God, should be seen as the supreme arbiter of the will of God is of the greatest significance to Matthew both theologically and practically. His church is, as we shall discuss in chapters three and four, embroiled in conflict with contemporary Pharisaic Judaism. Both sides acknowledge the law as the expression of the will of God. But each side interprets it quite differently. From the standpoint of Matthew's church, the interpretation Pharisaic Judaism gives the law results in the perversion of the will of God. Through the authoritative teaching of Jesus Messiah, the Son of God, Matthew's church believes that the will of God has truly been revealed and the law properly interpreted. This explains two phenomena we find in the First Gospel. Positively, the Matthaean Jesus designates the response he calls upon his disciples to make to his teaching of the law and of the will of God as the righteousness that is "greater" than that of the "scribes and Pharisees" (5:20). Negatively, the Matthaean Jesus excoriates the Israelite leaders for their understanding and practice of the law. They are "hypocrites," for their works are evil (23:3, 13, 15, 16, 23, 25, 27, 29). They are "blind guides" who lead people to destruction (15:14; 23:16, 24). While concerning themselves with trivial matters, they neglect the weightier matters of the law: justice, mercy, and faithfulness (23:23). For the sake of their tradition of the elders, they transgress the law of God (15:3). In short, they fail to perceive that the deepest intention of God's law is not "sacrifice" but "mercy," or love (9:13; 12:7; 22:34–40).

Because Matthew's church sees in Jesus Messiah, the Son of God, the supreme arbiter of the will of God, Matthew stresses throughout his Gospel the permanently binding character of his teaching. This, finally, is the reason Matthew highlights the teaching of Jesus to the extent he does: it reveals the will of God for all time to come. As far as the activity of "preaching" goes, Jesus engages in this, but so do John, the disciples, and the post-Easter church. But in the case of "teaching," Jesus alone is the one who does this. So it is that Matthew never even intimates that John or the pre-Easter disciples "teach," and when the exalted Son of God commissions his church to go to the nations, it is no accident that what these followers are given to "teach" the nations is "all that *I* have commanded you" (28:20). For Matthew, Jesus Messiah, the Son of God, is in truth the one teacher of his church.

Thus far, we have made no mention of the parables of Jesus. In Mark, three references to teaching introduce the so-called parable chapter (4:1–2). Although 13:1–52, the Matthaean counterpart to Mark 4, contains some eight parables of Jesus,[21] Matthew studiously avoids suggesting that they represent "teaching" on the part of Jesus (cf. 13:1–3 with Mark 4:1–2). Why is this?

Matthew states in words of Jesus in the pericope on the reason for speaking in parables (13:10–17) that the Israelite crowds are unable to comprehend the parabolic speech of Jesus because they are blind, deaf, and without understanding. In line with this statement, therefore, Matthew does not characterize the parabolic speech of Jesus to the crowds as teaching because it constitutes an apology against Israel.

The third verb with which Matthew describes the public activity of Jesus in the summary-passages 4:23 and 9:35 (cf. 11:5) is "to heal" (*therapeuō*). Just as Jesus is not "Teacher" or "Preacher" in the First Gospel in the sense that these terms are titles of Majesty, so neither is he "Healer." To Matthew's way of thinking, the one who "teaches," "preaches," and "heals" with divine authority is, again, Jesus Messiah, the Son of God.

What is the significance in the First Gospel of the healing, or, to put the question more broadly, of the miraculous activity of the Son of God? With other biblical writers, Matthew shares the view that disease in people or upheaval in nature are symptoms of sin and of bondage to Satan. This is why there is a close relationship also in the First Gospel between "faith" and the "forgiveness of sins" on the one hand and healing and the calming of storms on the other (cf. 8:5–10, 23–27; 9:2–8, 20–22, 27–31; 14:22–33; 15:21–28). This is furthermore why the Matthaean Jesus boldly declares in one verse: "But if it is by the Spirit of God that I cast out demons, then the kingdom of God has come upon you" (12:28). Through the activity of healing and of exercising dominion over nature no less than through the activity of teaching and preaching, Matthew portrays Jesus as liberating people from the sphere of Satan's rule and bringing them into the gracious sphere of the rule of God. In one passage, Matthew follows Mark in depicting the exorcisms of Jesus as a "plundering" of the kingdom of Satan (12:22–30//Mark 3:22–27).

It is important to observe how Matthew does not use miracle-stories. He does not use them, for example, to "prove" the divine Sonship of Jesus. To Matthew, miracles are incapable of providing proof such as this. Twice in the Gospel he records that Jesus, having cast out a demon, is immediately accused by the Pharisees as having accomplished this, not by the power of God, but by the power of the prince of demons (9:32–34; 12:24). Or we may look at it this way: had Matthew thought that miracles were capable of proving the divine Sonship of Jesus, surely he would not have recounted the two stories that tell how the Israelite leaders witness miracles of Jesus only to ask him for a sign that will yet convince them that he is God's emissary to Israel (cf. 12:38 to 12:9–37; 16:1).

We said that the broad significance of the miracle-story is that it portrays Jesus as bringing to bear upon the ills of people and the disturbances in nature the gracious, saving power of God's eschatological rule. In chapters 8–9, Matthew demonstrates best the role that the miracle-story (where it does not function simply as supportive scenery for, say, a debate) plays in the Gospel.[22] In these chapters, Matthew gathers together a series of ten miracle-stories, edits them so as to place the accent on the direct speech between Jesus and his partners in dialogue, and embeds them in a framework that has to do mainly with the theme of "following" Jesus (cf. 8:1, 10, 18–22, 23; 9:9, 19, 27). These factors indicate that Matthew places the miracle-story in the service of his concept of discipleship, and the reason he does so is to make it relevant for the members of his church.

For Matthew's church, Jesus is the exalted Son of God and no longer the earthly Son of God. With divine authority, the earthly Son of God performed mighty "acts of power" (*dynameis*; cf. 11:20, 21, 23; 13:54, 58; 14:2). Similarly, the exalted Son of God, who resides in the midst of his church and to whom God has given all authority in heaven and on earth (1:23; 18:20; 28:18–20), can perform mighty "acts of power." He does so, and this is Matthew's argument in chapters 8–9, on behalf of the disciple in post-Easter times who approaches him worshipfully and prayerfully in the attitude of faith even as the characters in these miracle-stories are pictured as approaching him with their prayer-like requests in the attitude of faith. To put it succinctly, Matthew employs the miracle-story in chapters 8–9 to teach the members of his church that Jesus Messiah, the exalted Son of God, is ever near them with his saving power.

In respect to the overall flow of Matthew's gospel-story, we should notice in passing that, following 11:1, when Jesus becomes the rejected Messiah of Israel, Matthew continues to describe him as healing people in Israel, even great numbers (cf. 12:10–13, 15, 22; 14:14; 15:29–31; 17:14–18; 19:2; 21:14). Through his ministry of healing to Israel, Jesus Son of God shows that he is indeed Israel's Messiah despite the fact that his preaching and teaching have fallen upon obdurate hearts.

A final matter begs for consideration. Why is it that Matthew has Jesus deliver his first major sermon (chaps. 5–7), which is the example par excellence of his teaching, in the setting of the mountain (5:1)? Luke, by contrast, identifies the plain as the place where it is given (6:17). And, what is particularly striking, why does Matthew select exactly the mountain as the setting for Jesus' mass healing of people (15:29–31)? Practically speaking, what could be more inconsiderate than that the "many crowds" coming to Jesus should be forced to lead or to carry up the mountain "the lame, the maimed, the blind, the dumb, and many others" in order to place them at the feet of Jesus (15:30)?

The answer, of course, has nothing to do with logistics but with theology. A survey of the Gospel reveals that the only christological title Matthew associates with the setting of the mountain is the "Son of God" (cf. 4:3, 6 to 4:8; 14:23 to 14:33; 17:1 to 17:5; 28:16 to 28:19). Owing to its height, the mountain in biblical documents often connotes nearness to God and hence is a place where prayer and divine revelation take place. In the First Gospel, this setting also alludes to Jesus as the Son of God. Thus, in that Jesus "teaches" and "heals" the crowds from atop the "mountain," he is revealing himself to be Israel's Messiah, the Son of God, the one who speaks and acts in the stead of God.

The Mission of the Son of God

The second and third main parts of the topical outline of Matthew's Gospel have to do with the public activity of Jesus Messiah (4:17–16:20) and with his suffering, death, and resurrection (16:21–28:20). In Israel, Jesus Messiah, the Son of God, discharges a ministry of preaching, teaching, and healing (4:23–25; 9:35; 11:1–6). In an effort to capture the full sweep of Matthew's portrait of the Son of God in Israel, we shall trace in bold strokes Matthew's sketch of him throughout chapters 4:17–28:20.

Having been declared by God in the presence of John to be the Son of God (3:13–17) and having proved himself to be perfectly obedient to his Father's will (4:1–11), Jesus takes up residence in Capernaum (4:12–16) and embarks upon his public ministry to Israel (4:17). He, the Son of God, calls his first disciples (4:18–22), who through him become sons of God (5:9, 45; 13:38). Followed by them and attracting huge crowds (4:20, 22, 23–25; 5:1), he ascends a mountain, a setting that in itself alludes to his divine Son-ship and the divine authority with which he speaks and acts, and presents himself to his disciples and Israel as the Messiah of Word (5:1–7:29). Then, wandering in the area of Capernaum and travel-ing across the Sea of Galilee and back, he performs ten mighty acts of deliverance, in so doing setting forth the nature and the cost of dis-cipleship (8:1–9:34). At the height of his ministry, in order to gather the crowds, driven and harassed as sheep without a shepherd (9:36), he commissions the twelve disciples (10:1, 5) to a ministry modeled on his own, one of preaching and healing though not of teaching (10:1, 7–8). Although the ministry of the disciples to the "lost sheep" from the house of Israel (10:6) is motivated by his compassion for his people (9:36), the anticipated results are sketched in negative terms (10:5b–11:1).

As adumbrated by his missionary discourse, Jesus Messiah, the Son of God, is rejected by all segments of Israel (11:2–12:50). John the Baptist questions whether he is in fact the awaited Coming One (11:2–3, 6). "This generation" looks upon him as a glutton and drunkard, the friend of tax-collectors and sinners (11:19). The cities of Chorazin, Bethsaida, and Capernaum, in which he has done his mightiest miracles, refuse to be moved to repentance (11:20–24). In explanation of such rejection, Jesus invokes the will of his Father (11:25–26). Following this, the leaders of Israel attack him: they charge first his disciples and then him with breaking the law (12:2, 10); they plot his death (12:14); they accuse him of carrying out his ministry on the authority of Beelzebul, the prince of demons (12:24); and they demand from him a sign (12:38). Fi-nally, even his family appears to desert him, so that his disciples alone remain as those who are his real relatives, the ones who do the will of his heavenly Father (12:46–50).

The response of Jesus Messiah, the Son of God, to his total rejec-tion by Israel is a dual one. On the one hand, he declares that Israel has become hard of heart, and gives public demonstration of this by addressing the crowds in "parables," in speech they cannot compre-hend (13:2–3, 10–13). On the other hand, he turns his attention to his disciples (13:16–17, 36–52), interpreting his parables for them (13:18–23, 36–43) and, in general, revealing to them the mysteries of the kingdom of heaven (13:11).

By the close of his parable speech, the course that the ministry of the Son of God will take is no longer in doubt. Jesus continues to show himself to be Israel's Messiah, through his miracles (14:15–21; 15:32–39), especially those of healing (14:13–14, 34–36; 15:29–31). But although the "crowds" per se are not said to reject him, neither do they accept him, and in his home village of Nazareth the townspeople take offense at him (13:53–58). As for the Israelite leaders, the encounters he has with them do not rise above the level of acrimoneous debate (15:1–14; 16:1–4). Indeed, in the face of their propensity for violence against him (12:14), which is true of Herod Antipas as well (14:1–12), he withdraws to a deserted place (14:13) or into the regions of Tyre and Sidon (15:21) and hence momentarily avoids them (16:4). Among those in Israel, only the disciples comprehend that he is in truth the Messiah, the Son of God (16:13–20), and even they can be men of "little faith" (14:28–33; 16:5–12) and in need of clarification (15:15–20). Finally, in that he heals the Canaanite woman's daughter (15:21–28), he gives silent witness to the fact that one day gentiles will come to him in the faith that Israel has chosen to deny him.

Following Peter's confession that he is the Messiah, the Son of God, Jesus himself tells the disciples for the first time of the events that will mark the remainder of his ministry: it is God's will that he go to Jerusalem and there suffer, die, and on the third day be raised (16:21). Peter takes umbrage at this, but Jesus rejects his protestations as the temptation of Satan and informs the disciples that the way of the cross is not only his way but also that of anyone who would follow him (16:22–28). Then, to confirm the earlier confession of his divine Sonship and to exhort the disciples to attend to his teaching concerning his passion, Jesus is transfigured in the presence of Peter, James, and John atop a mountain while a voice declares him to be God's Son and bids the disciples to "hear him" (17:1–13). Thereafter, the disciples likewise learn of the great power of faith (17:14–20).

The second passion-prediction (17:22–23) and an exchange with Peter over the voluntary payment of the "half-shekel tax" (17:24–27) initiate Jesus' ecclesiological discourse to the disciples (18:1–35). His message is that loving concern for the neighbor and the spirit of forgiveness are to be the hallmarks of the community of believers in whose midst he, the Son of God, will ever be present (cf. 18:6, 10, 20, 21–22).

Leaving Galilee, Jesus undertakes at last the journey to Jerusalem, traveling into the regions of Judea across the Jordan (19:1). Huge crowds again follow him, and he heals the sick (19:2). At the same time, he debates with his opponents (19:3–12) and the rich young man (19:16–22), instructs his disciples largely about ethical matters (19:13–15; 19:23–20:16; 20:20–28), announces his impending passion a third time (20:17–19), and heals two blind men (20:29– 34). Next, surrounded by the crowds who hail him as the "Son of David," he enters into Jerusalem itself with great ceremony (21:1– 11). The tragedy, however, is that "Son of David" for the people means no more than that he is "the prophet . . . from Nazareth of Galilee" (21:11).

In Jerusalem, Jesus enters the temple and cleanses it, leaving that evening for Bethany (21:12–17). The next day, he returns to the temple, once again stressing on the way the power of prayer (21:18– 22). In the temple, through his teaching of the people (21:23), his debates with the leaders (21:23–27; 22:15–46), his parables against Israel (21:28–22:14), and his speech of woes against the scribes and Pharisees (chap. 23), he shows himself to be the Son of God who wields in the house of God the authority of God. When he leaves the temple, it is said to be "empty," which attests to the circumstance that God has chosen to replace it with his Son (23:38; 26:61; 27:51).

From the temple, Jesus goes to the Mount of Olives, where he delivers to his disciples his eschatological discourse (chaps. 24–25). Although he tells them of dire things to come, he also informs them that the task of his community of followers, despite dissension within and tribulation from without, is to preach the gospel of the kingdom throughout the world and to await in hope and watchfulness his sudden return in glory at the end of the age as the Judge of all.

With his passion at hand, Jesus Messiah, the Son of God, himself controls the events that bring him to the cross (cf. 26:1–2). Although he is innocent of wrongdoing (26:59–60; 27:4, 19), the chief priests and the elders of the people enlist the support of Pilate and of the crowds to see to it that he is put to death (chaps. 26–27). On trial before the Sanhedrin, the irony is that he is condemned to death for not disclaiming for himself the truth that he is the Messiah, the Son of God (26:59–66). Placed on the cross, he dies as God's obedient and trusting Son (27:38–44), and through his death he effects the forgiveness of sins (26:28), thus destroying the temple and bringing the sacrificial cult of Israel to an end (27:51). The Jewish saints who come forth from their tombs (27:52–53) and the Roman soldiers who confess him to be the Son of God (27:54) prefigure the post-Easter church of people of Jewish and gentile origin.

Not death but resurrection concludes the gospel-story. Raised from the dead by God (28:1–10) and exalted to all authority in heaven and on earth, Jesus Messiah, the Son of God, commissions his followers to make disciples of all the nations (28:16–20). This mission they can undertake in all boldness, for they may rest assured that he will abide with them to the close of the age (28:20).

Jesus as the Son of David

It stands to reason that if Matthew portrays Jesus Messiah in the main as the Son of God, his presentation of Jesus Messiah as the "Son of David" (*huios tou Dayid*) will be more narrow and restricted in scope. This is in fact the case. Still, the two titles should not be viewed as competing with each other. The reason is that, as we saw above, Matthew attributes as a matter of course messianic expectation associated with the house of David to Jesus precisely as the Son of God. For Matthew, Jesus Son of God is the royal Messiah from the line of David.

But if what is said of Jesus as the Davidic Messiah can be ascribed equally well to Jesus as the Son of God, why does Matthew bother at all to depict Jesus as discharging segments of his ministry as specifically the Son of David? The answer is that Matthew employs the title Son of David, not only in a positive sense to assert that Jesus does in truth stand in the line of David and fulfill messianic expectation associated with his house, but also apologetically, to underline the guilt that devolves upon Israel for not receiving the one in whom it especially was to find blessing and salvation. This will become obvious in what follows.

The restricted manner in which Matthew uses the title Son of David is plain to see. To begin with, "Son of David" is applied only to the earthly Jesus and not to the crucified and exalted Jesus. Second, the disciples do not relate to Jesus on the basis of this title, for never do they confess or even address him as the Son of David. Third, apart from Jesus' entry into Jerusalem, this title is associated exclusively with the activity of "healing"; never, for example, is Jesus described as "teaching" or "preaching" as the Son of David. And fourth, even in regard to the activity of healing, except for the "blind and lame" in the temple (21:14), it is only individuals and never large numbers of people who are made well by the Son of David. Mass healings, in turn, are regularly attributed to Jesus as the Son of God (cf., e.g., 4:23–25; 8:16; 9:35; 11:5; 12:15; 14:14; 15:29–31).

The apologetic coloration of the title Son of David is likewise apparent. The persons Jesus heals as Son of David are, respectively, two "blind men" (9:27–31), a "blind and dumb man" (12:22), the "daughter" of a gentile woman (15:21–28), an additional two "blind men" (20:29–34), and the "blind and lame" in the temple (21:14). These persons are the "no-accounts" in Israel, as are the "children" who hail Jesus as the Son of David in the temple (21:15) and the Canaanite "woman" who pleads the case of her daughter (15:21–22). As Matthew puts it, these "no-accounts" are able to "see" and "confess" what Israel will not, namely, that Jesus is its Messiah. As such, their example underlines the guilt that is Israel's for its repudiation of Jesus.

That there is indeed no recognition in Israel of Jesus as the Son of David is made abundantly clear by Matthew. The Israelite leaders witness the healing activity of the Son of David, but this only provokes them to anger (21:15) or motivates them to charge Jesus with being an emissary of Satan (9:32–34; 12:22–24). The crowds at least pose the question as to whether he is the Son of David, but the manner in which they frame it (in the Greek NT) requires a negative reply (12:23). When Jesus enters Jerusalem and the crowds do hail him as the Son of David, they explain that this title means no more to them than that he is "the prophet . . . from Nazareth" (21:9–11).

Accordingly, Matthew is certainly concerned to present Jesus as the Son of David, the royal Messiah sent to save Israel whom Joseph son of David adopts into his line. But Matthew sharply restricts the scope of this title, preferring to subsume it under the chief christological category of his Gospel, the title Son of God.

Jesus as Lord

Some students of the First Gospel maintain, on largely unexamined grounds, that "Lord," or "Kyrios" (*kyrios*), is the chief christological title with which Matthew operates.[23] The evidence, however, suggests that it is not nearly so imposing a title as this.

Matthew uses the term *kyrios* on at least three levels. At 27:63, for instance, purely conventional usage dictates that the Israelite leaders address Pilate with the equivalent of the English "sir." Theologically, it numerous times denotes "God" (cf., e.g., 4:7, 10; 5:33; 9:38; 11:25; 21:9, 42; 22:37; 23:39; 27:10; 28:2). And, of course, it also appears as a designation for Jesus.

When it refers to Jesus, Kyrios is, like "Son of God," a "confessional" title in the sense that it crosses the lips exclusively of the disciples or of those who come to Jesus in the belief he can heal or save (cf., e.g., 8:2, 21). The only exception to this is that the accursed in the scene of the Last Judgment are also pictured as addressing Jesus as "Lord" (cf. 7:21–23; 25:37).

Far from being the central christological title of the First Gospel, Kyrios is rather of the nature of an auxiliary christological title. By this we mean to say that it always refers beyond itself to some other, more definitive, title.

Thus, in any number of passages the disciples and people of faith who address Jesus as "Lord" are in reality calling upon him in his capacity as the Messiah, the Son of God (cf. 8:2, 6, 8, 21, 25; 14:28, 30; 16:22; 17:4, 15; 18:21; 22:43–45; 26:22). In other passages, he is called "Lord" in his capacity as the Son of David (cf. 9:28; 15:22, 25, 27; 20:30–31, 33; 21:3). And in still others, he is "Lord" in his capacity as the Son of man (cf. 7:21–22; 12:8; 24:42; 25:37, 44). In all of these cases, the function of the title Kyrios is that it connotes acknowledgment on the part of those who employ it that Jesus—again, in his capacity as Messiah Son of God, Son of David, or Son of man—is one of exalted station whom God has invested with divine authority.

Jesus as the Son of Man

The one christological title in the First Gospel that approximates in importance that of Son of God is "Son of man" (*huios tou anthrōpou*). How do the two titles relate to each other?

A concordance study of the terms Son of God and Son of man shows that on such matters as possessing authority, giving one's life for others, enduring mockery and abuse, dying, being raised, and being entrusted by God with dominion, Matthew's description of Jesus as the Son of man coincides with his description of Jesus as the Son of God. At the same time, whereas the term Son of man is only marginally significant in the First Gospel as a vehicle for setting forth the earthly activity of Jesus (it does not occur until 8:20), the title Son of God is not utilized at all as a vehicle for setting forth the activity of Jesus at the parousia.

Accordingly, aside from the return of Jesus at the end of the age, the ideas Matthew associates with both titles are to a great extent the same. This suggests that the difference between the two is more a matter of function than of content.

"Son of God" is what we have termed a "confessional" title. That is to say, unless it be in mockery or blasphemy (26:63; 27:40, 43), the only human beings other than Jesus himself who can utter it are the disciples (14:33; 16:16) and the confessing Roman soldiers (27:54), by revelation of God (16:17). The force of this title in Matthaean usage is that it conveys the deepest mystery of the person of Jesus, viz., that it is in him that God has drawn near with his eschatological rule to dwell with his people (1:23; 18:20; 28:20). In a word, the title Son of God is at the heart of the most exalted confession of Matthew's church; it discloses how this church "knows" Jesus in Matthew's own day.

By contrast, "Son of man" in the First Gospel is what we shall term a "public" title. The unbelieving crowds, the Israelite leaders, and the gentiles beyond the church in the age of Matthew do not perceive Jesus to be the Son of God. On the contrary, they, the "world," interact with the earthly or exalted Jesus as the Son of man.

For example, when Jesus refers to himself in the audience of the crowds or of his opponents during his public ministry to Israel, he consistently does so by means of the title Son of man (cf. 8:20; 9:6; 11:19; 12:8, 32, 40). When he tells his disciples, as in sayings like the passion-predictions, what his death will mean for the world specifically or what Judas, the Israelite leaders, and gentiles are about to do to him, he again speaks of himself as the Son of man (cf. 17:12,

22; 20:18–19, 28; 26:2, 24, 45; also 17:9; 12:40 and 28:11–15). When he describes himself following Easter as the Exalted One who will reign over the world and raise up in it sons of the kingdom, people who will join his church and confess him to be the Son of God, once more the title he employs is Son of man (13:37–38). And when he sketches for the disciples his future return in glory as Judge of all the nations of the world, he likewise points to himself as the Son of man (cf. 10:23; 16:27–28; 19:28; 24:27, 30, 37, 39, 44; 25:31; 26:64).

The pattern, therefore, is consistent: if Matthew views Jesus in his interaction with his disciples during his ministry and with his church following Easter as the Messiah, the Son of God, he views him in his interaction with the world, first Israel and then the gentiles, as the Son of man. Still, at the consummation of the age, when Jesus will appear visibly as the Judge and Ruler of the universe so that the whole world will see what until that time only the eyes of faith had ever been given by God to perceive, then, says Matthew, the distinction between Jesus as the Son of God and Jesus as the Son of man will fall away; indeed, at the consummation both church and world will behold Jesus in all the majesty of God as the Son of man.

However, this side of the parousia, contends Matthew, Jesus remains preeminently the Messiah, the Son of God. Insight that is born of divine revelation is superior to that which is based on purely human powers of observation (16:17). Hence, the title Son of God throughout this age "outranks" the title Son of man (16:13–20). Supremely the Son of man "then," Jesus, claims Matthew, is supremely the Son of God "now."

CHAPTER THREE

MATTHEW'S UNDERSTANDING OF GOD

The single most comprehensive concept in the First Gospel is the "kingdom of heaven (God)" (*basileia tōn ouranōn* [*tou theou*]). It denotes, we learned in chapter one, that "God rules (reigns)," so that the expression the "rule (reign) of God" is an accurate paraphrase of it. It is largely through the concept of the kingdom that Matthew sets forth his understanding of God.

We have seen that Matthew employs the chief structural feature of the Gospel, his topical outline, in order to draft his portrait of Jesus: his person (1:1–4:16), his public ministry (4:17–16:20), and his suffering, death, and resurrection (16:21–28:20). By the same token, it is mainly in connection with the second chief structural feature of the Gospel, his view of the history of salvation, that Matthew develops his concept of the kingdom of heaven.

We recall that Matthew, in his view of the history of salvation, distinguishes between the "time of Israel (OT)" as the time of prophecy and the "time of Jesus (earthly—exalted)" as the time of fulfillment. Moreover, he also divides the broad time of Jesus, extending from birth to parousia, into discernible segments: the ministries to Israel of John, of Jesus, and of the disciples, and the ministry of the church to the world following Easter. Now John, Jesus, and the disciples all proclaim that the "kingdom of heaven is at hand" (3:2; 4:17; 10:7), and both Jesus and the church following Easter proclaim the "gospel of the kingdom" (4:23; 9:35; 24:14; 26:13). The focal point of all such "kingdom-proclamation," of course, is the activity of God in Jesus Messiah, his Son. In terms of the central thought controlling the First Gospel, such divine activity is to be understood as God's drawing near with his eschatological rule in the person of his Son Jesus to dwell to the end of the age with his people, the church (1:23; 18:20; 28:20).

In this chapter, we want to examine various aspects of the eschatological rule of God, or the kingdom of heaven, as Matthew describes it. At the same time, we must keep in mind the essentially christological orientation of this theological concept: Matthew insists that, short of the parousia of Jesus Son of man, it is in Jesus Messiah, the Son of God, that one encounters the kingdom of heaven.

The Kingdom of Heaven

Although the expression "the kingdom of heaven" (Hebrew: *malkuth shamayim*) does not occur as a fixed phrase in the OT, conceptually its roots are embedded there. The idea that "God rules," that he is "King," is one of Israel's elemental affirmations (cf. Exod. 15:18; Deut. 33:5; Pss. 47:2; 93:1; 96:10; 103:19; 145:13).

According to first-century Jewish thought, God's kingly rule is "eternal" and encompasses the entire world and all of the nations and powers in it. In the present age, however, God's sovereignty is fully acknowledged only in Israel. Still, the day is rapidly approaching when God will suddenly break into history, openly manifest himself in splendor as the Ruler of all, and in so doing free his people from heathen bondage and subject all nations to his holy will.

To turn to the First Gospel, our task is to discuss the "salvation-historical," the "cosmic," and the "ethical" dimensions of Matthew's concept of the kingdom of heaven.

The Salvation-Historical Dimension of the Kingdom

The salvation-historical dimension of the kingdom of heaven refers to the fact that, for Matthew, the kingdom is a transcendent, eschatological reality that confronts people already in the present but will be consummated only in the future. Thus, Matthew, as we observed, pictures John, Jesus, and the disciples as proclaiming in Israel that the "kingdom of heaven is at hand (*ēggiken*)" (3:2; 4:17; 10:7). The verb *ēggiken* denotes a "coming near," an "approaching," that is spatial or temporal in character. "Spatially," the kingdom has drawn near because God in the person of his Son even now resides with those who live in the sphere of his rule (1:23; 18:20; 28:20). Under the aegis of the earthly and exalted Son of God, the will of the Father who is in heaven above is not hidden but known on earth, and the disciples of Jesus respond to it with lives that reflect the greater righteousness (5:17–20; 6:10, 33; 11:25–27; 12:50; 16:19; 18:18; 28:18).

"Temporally," too, the kingdom of heaven has drawn near. Although the kingdom, to Matthew's way of thinking, belongs to the future, in the person of Jesus Son of God it has come upon the present so as radically to qualify it (3:2, 11–12; 4:17; 10:7; 11:2–6; 13:16–17). Consequently, the present is to be viewed in the light of the future and everything seen as moving towards the consummation and the parousia of Jesus Son of man (cf. 5:3–10; 13:39–40, 49; 24:3; 28:20).

The "spatial" and the "temporal" aspects of the drawing near of the kingdom of heaven are part and parcel of its "eschatological" nature. Associated with this adjective are notions about both the time and the ultimate significance of the kingdom. Matthew, for example, holds the kingdom of heaven to be an eschatological reality because the proclamation of its nearness occurs in the "time of Jesus (earthly—exalted)," the "last times" which precede the consummation and are inaugurated by the birth of Jesus (1:23) but which first burst upon Israel when John the Baptist "in those days" begins his ministry (cf. 3:1–2; 4:17; 10:7; 24:3, 14).

But the kingdom is also an eschatological reality in Matthew's perspective because the proclamation of its nearness is of ultimate significance for both Israel and the gentiles. The thrust of this proclamation is, after all, that God with his rule has in fact drawn near to humankind in his Son. In such proclamation, Israel and the nations encounter the rule of God, a rule that, again, is tending towards its consummation. God's will is that the proclamation of his kingdom be received with understanding, or faith, and that people enter the sphere of his sovereignty to their salvation. They can, however, reject the word and at the last perish.

With our discussion thus far, we have already gone some distance in explaining that the kingdom of heaven is a reality that can only be described in terms of both the present and the future. Indeed, the verb ēggiken, mentioned above, harbors within it this very tension between present and future. On the one hand, it connotes that the kingdom is indeed near, so near that in the person of the earthly and exalted Son of God the authority (power) of God impinges upon the present and decisively qualifies it. On the other hand, it connotes that the kingdom has not yet arrived, for God has not yet miraculously consummated his rule in all power and outward splendor. When will this take place? As the apocalyptic Son-of-man sayings stipulate, this will take place at the end of the age when Jesus Son of man returns for judgment.

If the verb *ēggiken* at 3:2; 4:17; and 10:7 embodies a tension between the present and the future modes of the kingdom, in numerous places in the Gospel the stress is more clearly on either the one pole or the other. Matthew, for example, in a wide variety of ways gives expression to his conviction that in the recent past God has been, and is presently, at work in his Son to visit people with his rule. It is this conviction that prompts him to utilize the eschatological phrase "[in] those days" and the schema of prophecy and fulfillment, especially as the latter is applied in the case of the formula quotations. It is likewise this conviction that motivates Matthew to attribute to Jesus divine authority, so that he delivers the Sermon on the Mount as the Son who stands above Moses (chaps. 5–7) and also dares to forgive sins (cf. 9:2, 5–6), incurring thereby the charge of blasphemy (9:3).

Matthew furthermore points to the presence of the kingdom in Jesus through his appropriation from the tradition of a number of eschatological images. Pertinent are the following. The Matthaean Jesus declares that "something greater" than either Jonah or Solomon is here (12:41–42). He warns that one should not attempt to place a "piece of unshrunk cloth" on an old garment (9:16) or to put "new wine" in old wineskins (9:17). He designates himself in quotation of the OT as the "Shepherd" (26:31) and describes his mission in terms of gathering the flock (cf. 15:24; also 2:6; 9:36; 10:6). He refers to himself also as the "bridegroom" (9:15) and to his time as one of joy and celebration as at a wedding (cf. 9:15; 11:19; 22:1–10). And he anticipates the eschatological banquet (cf. 8:11; 26:29) by granting table fellowship to tax-collectors and sinners (cf. 9:10; 11:19).

In connection with the matter of eschatological imagery, one word for which Matthew shows great affinity is *makarios* ("blessed"). This word, which portrays the present in the light of the future and hence attests to the tension between the two in Matthew's understanding of the rule of God, nevertheless bears strong witness to the kingdom as a present reality in that it expresses the unique religious joy that springs from those who share in the salvation God bestows upon all who live in the sphere of his sovereignty. These people are "blessed," for they have not taken offense at Jesus Messiah (cf. 11:6) but have received in faith the revelation imparted by his Father to the effect that he is the Son of God (cf. 16:17). Because of this, they can be said to have eyes that see and ears that hear the many things the prophets and righteous ones desired to see and hear but were not privileged to do so (13:16–17). In point of fact, these people are like faithful slaves who do the will of their lord (24:45–47), who reflect in their lives the eschatological reversal of values (cf. 5:3–9), and who rejoice in the face of persecution, knowing that their reward lies with God and that in enduring affliction they are following in the footsteps of the OT prophets (cf. 5:10–12).

Last, there are yet three passages in the First Gospel which, owing to the intensity with which they depict the kingdom as a present reality, merit special attention. The one passage we have in mind is 12:28. In substance, it underlines an important truth we have not yet mentioned, namely, that the rule of God effects the destruction of the rule of Satan. Of equal interest, however, is the circumstance that Matthew does not hesitate in this verse to make the kingdom the subject of a verb in the past (aorist) tense: "The kingdom of God 'has come' (ephthasen) upon you." In the whole of the Gospel, this passage represents one of Matthew's most direct overtures to "realized" eschatology.

The second passage is 21:43. Here "the kingdom of God" functions as the subject of a double predicate. As a saying of the earthly Jesus, the two verbs have been cast in the future tense, but the thing to note is that, from Matthew's vantage point in history, they refer to an event of the immediate past. At any rate, this saying ascribes to the kingdom such a degree of reality in the present that it can "be taken away" (arthēsetai) by God from Israel and "be given" (dothēsetai) to another nation that will produce its fruits.

The third passage is 11:12. As before, the kingdom is the subject of the sentence, but this time the verb is in the present tense (biazetai). As to its meaning, 11:12 is difficult to interpret, but the following translation seems to capture its intention: "From the days of John the Baptist until now the kingdom of heaven has suffered violence, and violent ones plunder it." Who, specifically, are these "violent ones"? As we have suggested elsewhere, from Matthew's perspective they are the devil and all the false Christians, Israelites, and gentiles who are his "sons" ("the sons of the Evil One"), those who resist the rule of God and "plunder" it in that through various means they lead "sons of the kingdom" astray and bring them to fall (cf., e.g., 7:15–23; 12:45d; 13:19–21, 38–39, 49; 23:13; 24:9–11; 25:41–46). Be that as it may, what is noteworthy about 11:12 is the circumstance that it describes the kingdom as a sphere that is present among people in such measure that it can be said to be vulnerable to attack from the side of its enemies.

If Matthew emphasizes the fact that God is presently at work in his Son to bring his eschatological kingdom to people, he sketches with even greater vividness the future consummation of the kingdom. In this regard, the primary figure, as we saw last chapter, is no longer Jesus Son of God but Jesus Son of man.

In our study of the titles of Jesus, we noted that Matthew's use of the terms Son of God and Son of man is controlled by one principle in particular: whereas the disciples of Jesus confess him to be the Son of God, the "public" (or "men") knows him as the Son of man (cf. 16:13 with 16:16; 14:33). In line with this principle, Matthew pictures Jesus following Easter as, on the one hand, residing in the midst of his disciples as the Son of God (cf. 28:20; also 18:20) but, on the other, as standing before the world as the Son of man (cf. 13:37–38a).

Now in terms of "kingdom-talk," Matthew quite easily extends this latter thought to the point where he depicts the world in post-Easter times as "the kingdom of the Son of man" (13:41), that is to say, as the realm over which the Son of man rules. Then, too, what the Son of man does, says Matthew, is to raise up in the world "sons of the kingdom" (13:38), people who are led by the world-wide missionary effort of the church to become disciples of Jesus and so to join the ranks of those who confess him to be the Son of God (16:16–17; 24:14; 26:13; 28:18–20). At the same time, Matthew's notion of the kingdom of the Son of man seems to be grander yet: this kingdom will not be limited to this age but will exist beyond the parousia (cf. 16:28). In other words, the idea that the term kingdom of the Son of man appears to express for Matthew is that following Easter God reigns over the world in the person of Jesus Son of man and, beyond the parousia, will continue to reign through his agency.

But having said this, we dare not fail to observe that the term kingdom of the Son of man is not without nuance in the First Gospel. It is a "public" term in the sense that it is oriented towards the world at large and treats of God's rule in the person of Jesus as it impinges upon the universe. By contrast, when Matthew speaks of the rule of God in the person of Jesus as it impinges upon the church this side of the parousia, he never makes reference to the kingdom of the Son of man but to the divine authority and the abiding presence with his disciples of Jesus Son of God. Of course at the parousia, when the eyes of the world will behold what until then only the eyes of faith can perceive, then, claims Matthew, the division between the church and the world concerning the mystery of the person of Jesus will cease to exist, and Jesus will openly exercize divine dominion in splendor as the Son of man.

Keeping these distinctions in mind, we turn to Matthew's description of the future kingdom. As he sees it, the event that inaugurates it will unfold in the following sequence: the forces of nature will suddenly fall into disarray, Jesus Son of man will be seen coming on the clouds of heaven in power and great glory, all the nations will be gathered before him, he will separate them into two groups, and he will pronounce judgment on them, thus determining who will "inherit the kingdom" that has been prepared from the foundation of the world and who will "go away into eternal punishment" (25:31–46; 13:40–43; 16:27; 24:29–31, 37–39, 44, 50).

Matthew is at pains in painting his portrait of the future kingdom to show that it is continuous with God's kingly activity in the present. The parables of the tares, mustard seed, leaven, and net illustrate this well. Thus, although the major point of the parable of the tares (13:24–30) is that darnel and wheat are to be allowed to grow side by side until the harvest (13:30a), it is none the less from the sowing of the seed by the farmer (the ministry of Jesus Son of God) that the harvest (the consummation of the age and the inauguration of the future kingdom by Jesus Son of man) finally results. The twin parables of the mustard seed (13:31–32) and of the leaven (13:33) put it this way: from something most insignificant, like a mustard seed or a little lump of leaven placed in dough (the ministry of

Jesus), there issues something most magnificent, like the mustard "tree" or the great mass of fully leavened bread (the future kingdom). The parable of the net (13:47–50) advances this truth as follows: the gathering of the fish (the growth of the church in this age owing to its missionary proclamation of the kingdom) is necessarily followed by the separation of the fish (the church, too, will undergo judgment at the consummation).

As far as Jesus himself and the righteous are concerned, Matthew shows that the future kingdom means, respectively, vindication and the perfect realization of hope. With respect to Jesus, the irony is that the Son of man who suffers crucifixion at the hands of Jew and gentile and is utterly rejected is the very One whom God has chosen to return at the consummation as the Judge and Ruler of all (cf., e.g., 17:22–23; 20:17–19; 13:41–43; 16:28; 25:31–46). To Jesus as well the saying applies. "For there is nothing hidden which shall not be revealed . . ." (10:26).

For the righteous, Matthew brings into play a wide variety of word-pictures in order to characterize the future kingdom as the perfect realization of hope. Matthew depicts the future kingdom, for example, as a realm the righteous will "enter" (5:20; 7:21; 18:3; 19:23–24; cf. also 23:13), "go into" (21:31), or "inherit" (25:34), and what these idioms signify is evident from parallel passages that tell of "entering life" (18:8–9; 19:17), "entering the joy of your Lord" (25:21, 23), or "inheriting eternal life" (19:29). Of course the contrary is equally true: one can "not enter" (5:20; 18:3; 23:13), be shut out (25:10), or be "thrown out" (8:12; 13:42, 50; 22:13; 25:30) and therefore excluded from the latter-day kingdom. In addition, the bliss the righteous will experience in the future kingdom is described in figurative language that refers to Jesus as the eschatological "bridegroom" (25:6, 10), to the consummated kingdom as a "wedding celebration" (25:10) or as a banquet (8:11; 26:29), and to the righteous as perfected ones who "shine as the sun" (13:43). And the reception of the "reward" that the future kingdom connotes for the righteous comes to expression in all those sayings that dwell on the reversal of their condition: he who loses his life will find it (10:39); the last will be first (19:30; 20:16); he who humbles himself will be exalted (23:12); and the radical changes enumerated by the Beatitudes (cf. 5:3–10).

The overall purpose of this discussion has been to set forth the salvation-historical dimension of Matthew's concept of the kingdom of heaven. This dimension dominates the concept, and one facet of it we have yet to cover more thoroughly is the crisis that the nearness of the kingdom precipitates for persons, whether Israelite or gentile. Still, what we have learned is that Matthew regards the kingdom of heaven as an exclusively eschatological reality: it is openly proclaimed by John, Jesus, the disciples, and the church in the "time of Jesus" (the "last times"), and such proclamation of the kingdom is of ultimate significance for Israel and for the nations. In other respects, the kingdom is a reality that is at once present and future: from the unprecedented activity of God in the person of Jesus in the present there will issue in the future the consummated kingdom of heaven. Christologically, the kingdom draws near in the present in the person of Jesus Messiah, the Son of God, and those who accept the gospel of the kingdom join the community of his disciples and experience the rule of God under his aegis. At the same time, these disciples also know that this same Jesus stands before the world as the Son of man, that in post-Easter times he works through his ambassadors to lead people in the world to know and confess him as the Son of God, and that at the end of time he, as Judge and Ruler of all, will inaugurate the future, splendid kingdom to the salvation of the righteous and the damnation of the wicked. Accordingly, the arrival of the future kingdom means the "public" vindication of Jesus, the one crucified and rejected, and, for the righteous, the perfect realization of their hope.

The Cosmic Dimension of the Kingdom

The cosmic dimension of Matthew's concept of the kingdom of heaven has to do with the oft-maligned notion of the "growth" of the kingdom. On this score, however, it should go without saying that the old liberal idea that the kingdom is to be regarded as a social, moral, or spiritual force that will gradually spread throughout the world as it captures the hearts of people, is foreign to the mind of Matthew. Moreover, from one standpoint Matthew, too, would reject any suggestion that the kingdom could be said to grow: he, like his Jewish contemporaries and Israelite predecessors, believes that God is, and always has been, the "Lord of heaven and earth" (11:25; cf. also 6:25–32; 10:29–30).

The thought that the kingdom grows relates to Matthew's understanding of the course of the kingdom in the world as a present reality that confronts people in the "time of Jesus." As Matthew sees it, God in heaven reigns indeed over all things, but he has determined in the last times to draw near to humankind in the person of Jesus Messiah, his Son. Still, the nearness of God in the person of his Son and, by extension, in the church's post-Easter proclamation of the gospel of the kingdom, is not something unambiguous. On the contrary, it is something that can be perceived only by means of divine revelation (13:11; 16:16–17). Nevertheless, as the church in post-Easter times proclaims the gospel of the kingdom to the nations (24:14; 26:13; 28:18–20), persons will in truth be led to acknowledge the rule of God in Jesus, his Son, and, as they become disciples of Jesus, the kingdom can in fact be described as growing. Finally, at the consummation of the age, God in the person of Jesus Son of man will wondrously establish his rule in glory over all the "tribes of the earth" (24:30). Accordingly, the course of the kingdom in the world during the "time of Jesus" is that from the "small beginnings" of Jesus Messiah, the Son of God, and his initial disciples (cf. 4:17; 10:7), the kingdom, through the agency of the post-Easter church (13:47; 28:18–20), "grows" as the gospel is proclaimed to the nations, and, at the last, when Jesus Son of man shall burst into history, this kingdom will visibly be established over all.

Several parabolic units in the Gospel document this view of the growth of the kingdom particularly well. In the parable of the mustard seed (13:31–32), for instance, the "mustard seed," which was proverbial among the Jews as the most minute of quantities, is depicted as "growing" until, miraculously, it becomes a "tree" in which the birds from heaven nest, an image which in the OT stands for a mighty empire (cf. Dan. 4:10–12, 21; Ezek. 31:6). In the parable of the leaven (13:33), the image is that of the little lump of "yeast" causing the dough to swell until the "whole" mass has become fully leavened. In the parable of the net (13:47–50), the "drag-net" is described as "gathering in" fish of every kind until that time comes when the good fish must be separated from the bad. In the interpretation of the parable of the tares (13:36–43), the text identifies the "field" over which the Son of man at the consummation will suddenly be revealed as ruling with the entire "world" (*kosmos*). And in the so-called parable of the last judgment (25:31–46), the Son of man is portrayed as seated on the throne of his glory with all the nations of the earth standing before him in acknowledgment of his universal rule. As we stated above, from small, seemingly insignificant, beginnings Matthew pictures the kingdom as, ultimately and miraculously, cosmic in scope.

The Ethical Dimension of the Kingdom

By the ethical, or personal, dimension of Matthew's concept of the kingdom of heaven is meant the new life that can result from a person's encounter with the reign of God. Of course the occasion for such encounter is, again, the presence of the kingdom in Jesus Messiah, the earthly and exalted Son of God, and therefore in the proclamation by him and his church of "the gospel of the kingdom."

In a number of passages, Matthew makes it clear that encounter with the earthly Jesus placed a person in a crisis of decision (4:17; 10:34–35; 11:3–6, 14–15, 20; 13:9, 43b; 21:31–32). As for his own time of the church, encounter with the gospel of the kingdom precipitates the same crisis (10:18; 24:14; cf. also 10:14, 20, 27, 40; 23:34). In confrontation with the words and deeds of the earthly Jesus, a person faced the choice of "repenting" and "entering" the gracious sphere of the kingdom (cf. 4:17; 11:20; 21:31–32) or of rejecting Jesus as the Messiah (cf. chaps. 11–12). In confrontation with the church's proclamation of the gospel of the kingdom, a person either "understands" the word (cf. 13:23) and is "baptized" (cf. 28:19) and observes all that Jesus has commanded (cf. 13:23; 28:20), or he does "not understand" the word and hence falls under the power of Satan (cf. 13:19, 38c–39a). Whoever understands the gospel of the kingdom may be compared to a "good tree" which produces "good fruit" (7:16–20; 12:33) or to a "good man" who brings forth "good things" out of his "good treasure" (12:35), that is to say, this person, like Jesus Son of God himself (cf. 26:42), "does the will of the heavenly Father" (cf. 6:10; 7:21; 12:50). As such a one, he abounds in righteousness more than the scribes and Pharisees (5:20) and will, at the coming of Jesus Son of man, be identified by him as one of the "righteous" (13:43, 49; 25:37, 46) who will "inherit eternal life" (25:46) and "shine [in perfection] as the sun in the kingdom of their Father" (13:43).

On the other hand, those who have fallen under the power of Satan are "evil ones" (cf. 13:19, 38c–39), who may be compared to a "bad tree" which produces "bad fruit" (7:17–18; 12:33) or to an "evil man" who brings forth "evil things" from his "evil treasure" (12:35). At the latter day the Son of man will designate these people as the "accursed" (25:41), and they will be cast into the "fiery furnace" (13:42; 25:41) or into the "outer darkness" (8:12) where they will experience "eternal punishment" (25:46), such as the "weeping and gnashing of teeth" (8:12; 13:42, 50). So again, encounter with the kingdom means that a person must decide: will he enter the "narrow gate" and take the "hard way" that leads to "life," or will he enter the "wide gate" and take the "broad way" that leads to "destruction" (7:13–14)?

With this delineation of Matthew's understanding of the ethical, or personal, dimension of the kingdom, we have treated in general Matthew's concept of the kingdom of heaven. Our concern now is to discuss the kingdom as it relates, respectively, to the kingdom of Satan, to Israel and to the nations, and, next chapter, to the church.

The Kingdom of Heaven and
the Kingdom of Satan

Matthew's concept of the kingdom of heaven involves a pronounced dualism that pits Satan against Jesus both as Messiah, Son of God, and as Son of man. The following is an attempt to sketch this.

Matthew's portrait of the arch-adversary of Jesus is that of a transcendent being who stands in unmitigated opposition to the kingdom of heaven (cf., e.g., 6:10, 13; 11:12; 12:24–29; 13:39). A striking feature is the plethora of names by which he is known. There is, for example, the term "Satan," which is a proper noun and the equivalent of the common noun "devil." In addition, Matthew also refers to Jesus' arch-adversary as the "Tempter" (4:3), "Beelzebul" (12:24, 27), the "Evil One" (13:19), and the "Enemy" (13:39).

Matthew describes Satan, in his opposition to the kingdom, as one whose power is superseded only by God and Jesus themselves. Thus, Matthew attributes to Satan a "kingdom" (12:26), which means that he, too, is looked upon as one who rules in the universe. Moreover, under his control are such supernatural beings as "angels" (cf.

25:41) and "demons" (cf. 10:8; 12:24), or "unclean spirits" (cf. 10:1). Of course, he also enjoys the fealty of humans (cf. 13:38c), and a major way in which he brings his power to bear upon them is through temptation: he endeavors to get them to act or to live "lawlessly" (cf. 7:23; 13:41; 23:28; 24:12), that is to say, in a manner which is contrary to the will of God (cf. 4:1–11; 6:13; 16:23; 27:40). For this reason he is called the "Tempter" (4:3) and the "Evil One" (cf. 6:13; 13:19).

Since Matthew shows that the kingdom of heaven draws near to people in the person of Jesus Messiah, the Son of God, it is not surprising that in the First Gospel Jesus himself should be the primary target of Satan. Indeed, the first time Satan is directly mentioned is in connection with his desire to tempt Jesus to disobedience and hence to the forfeiture of his divine Sonship (4:1–11). In this confrontation, however, Jesus proves himself to be superior to Satan (cf. 4:4, 7, 10–11). But although defeated by Jesus, Satan continues to wield power in the world. As a result, both the kingdom of heaven and the kingdom of Satan possess in the First Gospel the quality of "already . . . but not yet," though with opposite tendencies: on the one hand, Satan has already been overcome by the power of the kingdom of heaven at work in Jesus, but his capacity for evil has not yet been taken from him; on the other hand, the kingdom of heaven has already entered the world in Jesus the Son so as to challenge the rule of Satan, but it has not yet been established in splendor to Satan's destruction and the total elimination of evil.

The clash between Satan and Jesus Son of God in the First Gospel is an ongoing one. Satan is characterized as "the strong man" and Jesus Son of God, in that he casts out demons by the Holy Spirit and brings people into the sphere of God's reign, as the one who "binds" him and "plunders his goods" (12:28–29; cf. also 8:29). Conversely, Satan and those who do his bidding are depicted as doing violence to the kingdom of heaven and as "plundering" it (11:12). A case in point is Satan's enlistment of Peter in an effort to put Jesus at cross-purposes with his Father and to turn him away from the path that leads to the cross (16:21–23). It is precisely to fend off onslaughts of Satan such as this that Jesus teaches his disciples to pray (6:13): "And lead us not into temptation, but deliver us from the Evil One" (or: "from evil"). On another level, Satan also exercises his malevolent will against Jesus through the Israelite crowds (cf. 11:16; 12:39, 45; 16:4) and their leaders (cf. 16:1; 19:3; 22:18, 35; 23:15), who ask Jesus for a sign or who tempt him, not the least while he is hanging on the cross (27:39–43). Indeed, through a parable of Jesus Matthew makes the programmatic observation that Satan is the personal "Enemy" of Jesus Messiah, who has usurped in in Israel the allegiance that is due Jesus alone (13:24–30). Nevertheless, as the story of the temptation at the beginning of the Gospel adumbrates, the repeated attacks of Satan are not sufficient to induce Jesus to divest himself of his divine Sonship and to bring him from his mission (cf. 16:21).

As the arch-adversary of Jesus Messiah, the Son of God, it follows that Satan should also be portrayed in the First Gospel as endeavoring in post-Easter times to destroy his church. Externally, he attempts this through the persecution and affliction of the church by Jews and gentiles (cf. 13:39a and 5:44 to 5:10–12; 10:17–18, 22–23, 28; 23:34; 24:9). But he is active inside the church as well. For example, Satan subverts the influence of the "word of the kingdom" upon persons who join the church but are without "understanding," or true faith, and so brings them under his sway. But in Matthew's eyes, the mark of those who serve Satan is above all contrariety to the will of God, or "lawlessness" (*anomia*; cf. 13:38c–39a, 41; 7:21–23; 24:12). This, in turn, comes to expression in any number of ways, such as in false speech (cf. 5:37), in a failure to be loving (cf. 20:15) or to be single-mindedly devoted to God (cf. 6:23), in lukewarmness towards the demands of discipleship (cf. 25:26), in an unwillingness to forgive a fellow-disciple (cf. 18:32, 35), and in sins of every kind against the second table of the law (cf. 15:19).

There is one circle within the church, however, to which Matthew calls special attention in warning his community against lawlessness, the so-called "false prophets" (cf. 7:15–23; 24:11, 24). The false prophets appear to be enthusiasts (cf. 7:22; 24:24), but the thing to note is that Matthew compares them to "rapacious wolves" (7:15) whose deeds are evil, or "lawless" (cf. 7:16–20, 23), and who lead many astray (24:11, 24). At the last, they will be denied entrance to the consummated kingdom of heaven (7:21, 23).

So far we have concentrated on Satan as the arch-adversary of

Jesus Messiah, the Son of God, and of his church. If, on the other hand, we shift our gaze to the "world," we encounter Satan as the transcendent antagonist of Jesus in his capacity as the Son of man. Whereas Jesus Son of man is said to be active in the world to raise up "sons of the kingdom," Satan is active in the world to raise up "sons of the Evil One" (13:37–39). As before, the mark of Satan's followers is "lawlessness" (13:41), and at the consummation of the age they will be cast into the "fiery furnace" (13:40, 42). This thought, in turn, leads us to the final point Matthew makes concerning Satan: his capacity for evil is restricted to the present age, and at the Last Judgment the Son of Man will consign him, his angels, and his "sons" to "eternal punishment" (25:41, 46).

In sum, therefore, Matthew's Gospel evinces a remarkable degree of dualism in its description of the kingdom of heaven and of the kingdom of Satan. The antagonists, Jesus and Satan, are locked in mortal combat, and the power of each is cosmic in scope, extending both to supernatural beings and to the world of humankind. At the same time, Jesus in his messianic ministry has in effect already defeated Satan, so that even though he can wreak havoc on the church, bringing disciples to fall, and raise up in the world those who will do his bidding, he cannot, finally, prevail. In the present time the power of the kingdom, which the exalted Son of God already wields, serves to strengthen the disciples in their struggle with Satan, and at the last, when the kingdom of heaven will be consummated in splendor, the Son of man will judge Satan and cast him and all who are his into the eternal fire.

One further matter calls for comment. In treating Matthew's satanology, we discover that it coincides perfectly with the pattern of his Christology. In the context, for example, of Jesus' earthly ministry and of Israel and of the church, Matthew pictures Satan as the antagonist of Jesus Messiah, the earthly and exalted Son of God. But in the context of the world and of the parousia, he pictures Satan as the antagonist of Jesus Son of man.

The Kingdom of Heaven and Israel and the Nations

We have just seen that Matthew views the nearness of the kingdom of heaven as a mortal threat to the rule of Satan. Furthermore, since he likewise holds that Satan is at work in both Israel and the world to effect his malevolent purposes, it becomes obvious that Matthew's position is that the kingdom of heaven must establish itself on earth in the face of concerted opposition from Jews and gentiles alike.

We recall that Matthew is eminently concerned to demonstrate that Jesus Messiah, the Son of God, in whom the kingdom of heaven draws near to humankind, is sent first of all to Israel (cf., e.g., 2:6, 15; 10:6; 15:24). Through his ministry in Galilee of teaching, preaching, and healing (4:17, 23–25; 9:35; 11:1–6), Jesus confronts the crowds with the kingdom. Their response, however, is one of rejection. They do not perceive who he is (cf. 13:13), and their leaders tempt him (16:1; 19:3; 22:18, 35), demand from him a sign (12:38; 16:1), accuse him of blasphemy (9:3; cf. also 26:65) and of breaking the law (12:10; cf. also 12:2; 15:2), and charge him with carrying out his ministry on the authority of the prince of demons (9:34; 12:24). Hence, the whole of Israel proves itself to be "an evil and adulterous generation" (cf. 12:39–45; 16:4; also 11:16; 17:17; 23:36) which refuses to repent and receive the kingdom of heaven (cf. 4:17 and 10:7 to 11:20 and 12:41).

The finality with which Israel rejects its Messiah and therefore the kingdom of heaven comes to light in the passion narrative. The animosity of the leaders of the people against Jesus is such that they plot his death and see to it that it takes place (cf. 12:14; 16:21; 21:45–46; chaps. 26–27). To this end, they secure the aid of Judas (cf. 26:20–25, 47–50; 27:3–4), of the crowds (cf. 26:47; 27:20–23), and of the gentile authorities (cf. 27:1–2, 11–38). In the presence of Pilate and at the foot of the cross, however, the crowds join their leaders in total condemnation of Jesus (cf. 27:15–26), and together these two groups function, ironically, as the acknowledged representatives of that people God had once chosen to be his own (cf. 27:25, 39–44). Finally, in regard to the Easter-event, although the truth of the matter is that God has raised Jesus from the dead, the Jews perpetuate the slanderous rumor that his disciples came by night and made off with his body (28:11–15).

Accordingly, Matthew depicts Jesus Messiah, the Son of God, as bringing the kingdom to his people Israel in his person and ministry and as being rejected by them. In addition, in looking back upon the years since Easter, Matthew can boast of no change in Israel's attitude towards Jesus. Indeed, in these years his church has been forced to separate itself from the Jewish community, and two indications of this in the Gospel are the twin circumstances that Matthew describes the synagogues Jesus visits as "their synagogues" (cf. 4:23; 9:35; 10:17; 12:9; 13:54; also 23:34) and treats the leaders of the people, whether "chief priests and elders" or "scribes and Pharisees" or "Pharisees and Sadducees," as though they had always formed as monolithic a front as do the leaders of the Pharisaic Judaism his church must face.

In charting the course of the recent past, therefore, Matthew shows that if Israel did not receive Jesus' proclamation of the gospel of the kingdom (4:23; 9:35), neither has it received the church's proclamation of the gospel of the kingdom (cf., e.g., chap. 10; 23:34). As can be seen from the example of its leaders, Israel steadfastly refuses to "enter . . . the kingdom of heaven" (cf. 23:13; 21:31). What is more, Israel has even responded to the missionary efforts of the church with persecution (cf. 5:10, 12, 44; 13:21).[24] Thus, disciples of Jesus, particularly "missionaries," are made to submit to such ill-treatment as verbal abuse (cf. 5:11), arraignment for disturbing the peace (cf. 10:17), perjured testimony in court (cf. 5:11), flogging in the local synagogue (cf. 10:17; 23:34), stoning (cf. 21:35), pursuit from city to city (cf. 10:23; 23:34), and even death (cf. 10:28; 21:35; 23:34). In consideration of all this, Matthew employs parables of Jesus to decry Israel under all of the following images: it is as unreceptive "soil" in which the seed of proclamation is unable to take root and bear fruit and so dies (cf. 13:3b–7); it is as "weeds" ("darnel") that are sown by the enemy of the farmer who sows good seed (cf. 13:24–30); it is as a "son" who does not repent of his duplicity towards his father and do his will (cf. 21:28–32); it is as "farmers" who lease a vineyard but refuse to pay rent and not only beat, kill, and stone the owner's slaves but murder his son as well (cf. 21:33–41); and it is as "guests" who are invited by a king to a wedding celebration for his son but make light of the invitation and seize, abuse, and kill the slaves of the king (cf. 22:1–8).

As for the leadership of Israel, Matthew is vitriolic in his condemnation of it. The Matthaean Jesus denunciates the "scribes and Pharisees" as "hypocrites" (cf. chap. 23) and charges them with all of the following: not only do they refuse to "enter" the kingdom themselves, but they also prevent others from "entering" it (cf. 23:13); they search out proselytes only to make of each one a "son of Gehenna" twice as much as themselves (cf. 23:15); they are blind guides who teach people to swear falsely (cf. 23:16–22); they concern themselves with trivia, neglecting the weightier matters of the law (cf. 23:23–24); outwardly they appear "clean" to people, but inwardly they are full of extortion (cf. 23:25–26); to others they seem righteous but in reality they are full of hypocrisy and lawlessness (cf. 23:27–28); while paying tribute to the prophets of old, they put to death and persecute those whom God sends to enlighten them (cf. 23:29–36); they esteem their own tradition of the elders more than the law of God (cf. 15:1–9); and they espouse an evil teaching of which one must beware (cf. 16:6, 11–12).

Finally, Matthew also attempts to address the question—how could it ever happen that Israel should become so blind and perverse? The one answer he gives we have already noted above: Israel has fallen under the rule of Satan. A second answer he gives is that God has ordained that Israel should not be made privy to the secrets of the kingdom of heaven, for which reason the people are "blind, deaf, and without understanding" (cf. 13:10–13; also 11:25). In the case of both of these answers, however, we should observe that there is no intention on the part of Matthew to excuse Israel for its rejection of Jesus and its persecution of the church. Quite the opposite, Matthew goes to great lengths to underline the guilt that devolves upon Israel for its failure to receive its Messiah: all Israel makes itself juridically responsible for the blood of Jesus (27:25); the leaders of the people themselves announce the punishment and loss the nation must endure for its treatment of the Son of God (21:37–41); and in words of Jesus Matthew declares that Israel is also culpable for its mistreatment of Christian missionaries (23:34–36).

What, then, has resulted from Israel's action? One result has been the destruction of Jerusalem (cf. 22:7). But this is only the physical manifestation of a second result, viz., that God, as Matthew puts it in a saying of Jesus, has chosen to "take away" his kingdom from Israel and to "give it" to a "nation" which will "produce the fruits of it" (21:43). The "nation," of course, is the "church" (cf. 16:18; 18:17), and the "kingdom" is the rule of God as a present reality (cf. 1:23; 18:20; 28:20). Consequently, owing to Israel's rejection of the proclamation of the gospel of the kingdom by Jesus Messiah, the Son of God, and by his ambassadors, God withdraws his rule from Israel and Israel ceases to be his chosen people.

Yet a third result of Israel's action is that the basic mission of Matthew's church is no longer to Israel per se (cf. chap. 10) but to the nations (cf. 22:9; 23:37–39; 24:14; 26:13; 28:18–20). Christian missionaries, as we have seen, are still at work in contemporary Israel (cf. 10:41; 23:34), but it is on the gentiles that the Matthaean church has now set its sights. Still and all, Matthew is under no illusions as to the reception the nations will give the gospel of the kingdom and the church's missionaries. Already in his day he reports in words of Jesus that disciples bear witness to the gentiles even as they are "dragged before governors and kings" (10:18), that the church is "hated by all the nations" because of its allegiance to Jesus (cf. 24:9; 10:22), that it suffers "tribulation" at the hands of gentile opponents (cf. 13:21; 24:9, 21, 29), and that members of the church are "killed" (cf. 10:28; 24:9). In view of such happenings as these, it is little wonder that Matthew should see Satan at work in the world raising up "sons of the Evil One" (cf. 13:38–39) or that he should boldly state through the mouth of Jesus that the nations, too, will undergo judgment at the consummation of the age (cf. 13:41–43; 25:41–46), and this precisely in terms of the way in which they have treated those who belong to the church (cf. 25:40, 45).[25]

To recapitulate, Matthew describes the kingdom of heaven as confronting Israel in the person of Jesus Messiah, the Son of God, and, following his death and resurrection, in the church's proclamation of the gospel of the kingdom. Israel, however, has responded negatively both to Jesus and, since Easter, to his church's missionary efforts. The upshot is that God has withdrawn his rule from Israel and now exercizes it in Jesus, the exalted Son of God, in the "empirical" sphere of the church. Israel, on the other hand, stands condemned, and the basic mission of the church is henceforth to proclaim the gospel of the kingdom among the nations. At the same time, the nations, too, are hostile to the message of the church, and Matthew warns that at the Latter Day they will likewise have to answer to the Son of man. But until that day, the task of the church is indeed to proclaim the gospel of the kingdom everywhere, and through this proclamation, in the face of opposition from Jew and gentile, God in Jesus, and in association with the church, visits people with his gracious rule.

With this summary, we have arrived at the place in our delineation of the thought of Matthew where we must speak at length about Matthew's understanding of the church. It is to this topic that we now turn.

CHAPTER FOUR

MATTHEW'S UNDERSTANDING
OF THE CHURCH

Because Israel has repudiated its Messiah, God, claims Matthew, has withdrawn his kingdom from it and given it to the church (21:43). The church, as the central thought of the Gospel defines it, is the community in which God in the person of his Son Jesus chooses to dwell to the end of the age ("God [is] with us," 1:23; cf. 18:20; 28:20). More specifically, this community is made up of those who, since Easter, have been called by Jesus through baptism to be his disciples (28:19). In contrast to Israel and to the gentiles, the church is the new "nation" God has raised up for himself (21:43), the "people" whom Jesus has saved from their sins (1:21). Within the flow of the gospel-story, the disciples who follow Jesus function both positively and by reverse example as "typical" of the members of Matthew's church. It is, therefore, by analyzing Matthew's portrait of the disciples that we gain insight into his understanding of the church.

The Nature of Discipleship

A distinctive feature of Matthew's portrait of Jesus is the unique relationship he enjoys with God (cf. 11:25–27). God is the Father of Jesus in a way not predicated to other human beings (1:22–23; 2:15; 3:17; 11:27; 17:5). Conversely, Jesus is the Son of God in a manner that is true of no one else (3:16–17; 11:27; 14:33; 16:16; 26:63–64; 27:54; 28:19). Nevertheless, when Jesus calls persons to follow him and therefore to become his disciples, Matthew shows that through him, the Messiah Son of God, they enter into a relationship of sonship with God.

So it is that Jesus designates his disciples in the First Gospel as "sons of God" (5:9), "sons of your heavenly Father" (5:45), and "sons of the kingdom" (13:38). By the same token, when speaking of God to the disciples, Jesus repeatedly refers to him as "your Father" (cf., e.g., the Sermon on the Mount: 5:16, 45, 48; 6:1, 4, 6, 8, 14, 18, 26, 32; 7:11) and even exhorts them to address him as "Father" in prayer (6:9). With an eye to himself, Jesus declares that his disciples are his true relatives (12:49) and his "brothers" (28:10), and tells the disciples that they, too, are all "brothers" (23:8; cf. 18:21, 35). In one passage in the Gospel, Matthew has Jesus stress at once his uniqueness in comparison with his disciples and his "relatedness" to them: "For whoever does the will of *my Father* in heaven is *my brother, and sister, and mother*" (12:50).

Matthew is at pains throughout his Gospel to emphasize in scenes that depict Jesus as interacting with his disciples both the uniqueness of Jesus as the Son of God and his close association with his disciples as sons of God and brothers. On the one hand, Jesus stands out from his disciples as the obvious figure of authority. The relationship he has with them is characterized as that of "teacher and learner," of "master and slave" (10:24–25). They regularly address him as "Lord," acknowledging thereby his exalted station and divine authority (cf., e.g., 8:21, 25; 14:28, 30; 16:22; 17:4; 26:22). Moreover, it is he who summons, dispatches, commands, and teaches, and it is they who follow, go, obey, and heed. For example, Jesus bids his first disciples to come after him, and they leave their nets at once and follow him (4:18–22; cf. also 8:21–22; 9:9). He ascends the mountain to teach, and they come to him as he sits (5:1–2). He embarks into the boat, and they step in after him (8:23; cf. 14:22). He summons the twelve for missionary instruction, and they attend to his words (10:1, 5; 11:1). He takes the lead in going through the grain fields, and they walk with him (12:1). He enters the house, and they approach him and hear the explanation of the parable of the tares (13:36). He gives the permission, and Peter walks on the water (14:28–29). He dispatches the two disciples, and they return with the animals on which he rides into Jerusalem (21:1–7). He determines where he will eat the passover, and they make the necessary preparations (26:18–19). He tells the women after he has been raised where his disciples are to meet him, and the disciples go to the mountain in Galilee to which he has directed them (28:10, 16).

On the other hand, Matthew also highlights the close association the disciples have with Jesus. Recently, Hubert Frankemölle has called attention to the importance in the First Gospel of the concept of "being with Jesus."[26] The Greek preposition translated as "with" (*meta* + genitive case) is frequently employed to denote accompaniment (cf., e.g., 12:3: "David . . . and those who were 'with him' "). Of great interest is the way in which Matthew carefully restricts the circle of those who share in the presence, or the company, of Jesus. Thus, if we take the Second Gospel for purposes of comparison, we discover that Mark depicts a broad spectrum of people as sharing in the company of Jesus: not only are Peter, James, and John (5:37, 40; 14:33) or the twelve (3:14; cf. 11:11; 14:17) or the disciples (3:7; 14:14) said to be "with Jesus" or he "with them," but it is also said, respectively, that Jesus eats "with sinners and tax collectors" (2:16), that other boats are "with him" as he journeys across the lake (4:36), that the demoniac whom he heals begs to be "with him" (5:18), that Jesus accedes to the plea of Jairus and goes "with him" to his sick daughter (5:22–24), and that Judas at the last supper eats "with me [Jesus]" (14:18).

In contrast to Mark, Matthew's presentation of those who are "with Jesus" or Jesus "with them" is far more limited in scope. Except for Mary his mother (2:11) and tax-collectors and sinners (9:11), the list extends only to Peter (26:69, 71; cf. 26:40), one of Jesus' followers (26:51), Peter and the two sons of Zebedee (26:37–38), and the twelve or eleven disciples (26:18, 20, 36; 28:20). Noticeably absent from this list are such as the crowds or their leaders or even Jairus and the healed demoniacs. Indeed, in the First Gospel Judas does not so much as eat with Jesus but merely dips his hand with him in the dish, in this manner marking himself as the one who will betray Jesus (26:23). In point of fact, Jesus is only "with Israel" as with a "faithless and perverse generation" from whom he will withdraw his presence (17:17), and the critical principle obtains: "He who is not *with me* is against me, and he who does not gather *with me* scatters" (12:30).

In the First Gospel, then, Jesus grants the privilege of his company almost without exception only to his own. Before Easter, these are his disciples. After Easter, they are his church (16:18). The disciples before Easter follow along "with Jesus" as he leads them to the cross and resurrection (cf. 16:21; 20:17–19). The church after Easter makes its way towards the consummation of the age and the parousia of the Son of man on the promise of the exalted Jesus that he will surely be "with them [you]" (28:20).

What such close association with Jesus means theologically Matthew explains in the key passages 1:23 ("Emmanuel . . . God [is] *with us*"), 18:20 ("there am I *in the midst of them*"), and 28:20 ("I am *with you* always"). It means, as the central thought of the Gospel also states, that through his presence Jesus Messiah, the earthly and exalted Son of God, mediates to his disciples or church the gracious, saving presence of God and his rule. Now if, in line with this truth, these three passages are examined in context, we see that they relate the presence and therefore the authority of the earthly and exalted Son of God to the basic activities characterizing not so much the ministry of the earthly disciples as that of the post-Easter church: baptizing (28:19), teaching (28:20), prayer (18:19), church discipline (18:18), and, in general, the mission to the nations (28:19). In addition, Matthew likewise reveals that the church's celebration of the Last Supper is done not only in commemoration of the shedding of the blood of the Son of God for the forgiveness of sins (cf. 26:28 to 27:38–54), but also in anticipation of that day to come when he will again drink wine "with them [you]" in the glorious kingdom of his Father (26:29). In short, Matthew utilizes the concept of "being with Jesus" and the related idiom of his "being with them" in order to restrict close association with Jesus almost exclusively to the circle of his disciples and, theologically, to set forth the truth that the church worships and carries out its ministry to the close of the age in the presence and on the authority of the exalted Son of God, through whom God exercizes his gracious, saving rule.

The Will of God

Accordingly, the disciples, in being called by Jesus to walk in his presence, become the recipients of divine grace (4:17–22). They are the "blessed" ones (5:3–11), those who are given to share in that unique religious joy that is indicative of the eschatological age of salvation which God's drawing near in his Son has inaugurated. They are the ones declared to be the "salt of the earth" (5:13) and the "light of the world" (5:14). As such, they follow along behind

Jesus, and he imparts to them his teaching (cf. 5:1b–2). They for their part respond to the gracious call of Jesus and to his teaching by leading lives that reflect the "greater righteousness" (5:20).

We recall from chapter two that the teaching of Jesus Messiah, the Son of God, has to do with the will of God in terms of its original intention (cf. 19:4, 8; 22:16). This teaching is binding on the church for all time to come, and the church discharges its own ministry of teaching in post-Easter times by rehearsing all that Jesus has commanded (28:20).

To speak of the will of God is to broach the question of Matthew's understanding of the law, which is a much disputed issue. For purposes of clarification, it should be observed that the term "law" (*nomos*), when used by itself in the First Gospel (5:18; 12:5; 15:6; 22:36; 23:23), does not refer merely to the so-called Ten Commandments but, more broadly, to the five books of Moses, or the Pentateuch. Similarly, the expression "the law and the prophets" denotes quite simply the whole of the OT as it is known to the church of Matthew and functions for it as Scripture (cf. 5:17; 7:12; 11:13; 22:40).

Now we know that Jesus, in Matthew's eyes, is the Messiah, the Son of God. What he teaches, we said, is the will of God in terms of its original intention. How this teaching of Jesus squares with the Mosaic law comes to light in the antitheses of the Sermon on the Mount (5:21–48), those peculiar sayings of Jesus which are characterized by some variation of the formula "You have heard that it was said to the men of old . . . but I say to you . . ." (5:21–22, 27–28, 31–32, 33–34, 38–39, 43–44).

Commentators do not agree on how to construe the antitheses. On one basic matter they divide themselves into two camps. On the one hand, some hold that Jesus in the antitheses only deepens, intensifies, or radicalizes at points the intention of the law of Moses.[27] On the other hand, others contend that, in certain of the antitheses, Jesus radicalizes the intention of the law of Moses to such degree that he abrogates it at points.[28]

To review the antitheses, scholars seem to agree that the first and second ones, on murder (5:21–26) and on adultery (5:27–30), merely intensify commands of Moses (cf. Exod. 20:13, 14). Moreover, a majority is likewise convinced that the sixth antithesis, on love of one's enemy (5:43–48), is also intended simply to radicalize a command of Moses (cf. Lev. 19:18). As for the fifth antithesis, on retribution (5:38–42), those scholars who take the position that Jesus in certain of the antitheses so radicalizes the law of Moses that he abrogates it all appear to agree that such is the case here. For whereas the Mosaic law regulates retribution but in so doing makes provisions for it (cf. Exod. 21:23–25; Lev. 24:19–20; Deut. 19:21), Jesus, they maintain, forbids it altogether. This leaves the third and fourth antitheses. What is to be made of them?

John Meier argues in a technical treatment of Matthew 5 that these antitheses, too, are to be seen as abrogating Mosaic injunctions.[29] With respect to the third antithesis (5:31–32), Jesus rescinds the permission for divorce that Deut. 24:1–4 presupposes and, in line with this, likewise annuls the command about the giving of the bill of divorce. The so-called "exceptive clause" of 5:32 ("except on the ground of *porneias*") allows for divorce, not by reason of "unchastity" (as the RSV, e.g., incorrectly translates *porneias*), but only in the event two people (e.g., gentiles joining the church) have, in violation of Lev. 18:6–18, entered into what must be judged to be an "incestuous marriage." So understood, the fourth antithesis does not provide a "loophole" for easy divorce (namely, adultery), but, on the contrary, is thoroughly radical in its prohibition of divorce.

Concerning the fourth antithesis (5:33–37), what Jesus revokes is the permission the law grants, as well as the obligation it in some instances enjoins, to make use of vows and oaths (cf. Exod. 20:7; 22:10–11; Lev. 19:12; Num. 5:19–22; 30:3, 16a; Deut. 6:13; 10:20; 23:21). The thrust of this antithesis is that vows and oaths are wrong because they infringe upon the majesty of God: he who is holy and ever truthful is made the guarantor of the alleged truth of sinful human beings.

Consequently, it would seem that the Matthaean Jesus, in the fifth antithesis for sure, and very likely in the third and fourth antitheses as well, does abrogate parts of the Mosaic law in the interest of promulgating more stringent injunctions. But if this is the case, how does abrogation of parts of the Mosaic law harmonize with the words of Jesus in 5:17–18, where he announces that he has "not come to abolish the law or the prophets . . . but to fulfill them," and that "till heaven and earth pass away, not an iota [yod], not a dot [stroke], will pass from the law"?

The answer, it appears, is that Matthew, as 11:13 indicates, sees the law and the prophets, the entire OT, as "prophesying," as pointing forward, to the events that mark the eschatological age of salvation. At the center of these events, of course, is Jesus Messiah, the Son of God. With his coming, in what he says and does, the law and the prophets attain to their "fulfillment" (5:17). The law that remains in force as long as heaven and earth shall last (5:18) is the law precisely as Jesus delivers it to his disciples and church. It is, properly understood, the messianic law. For none other than Jesus Messiah is the one who teaches the "way of God" with absolute truth and authority (22:16; 7:28–29) and hence stands above Moses: "You have heard . . . but I say to you." It is exactly his words that the church is to hear and do (7:24–27), and these words will never pass away (24:35). In brief, if for the Jews Moses is the supreme arbiter of the will of God, for the church it is Jesus Messiah, the Son of God. Accordingly, the law as Jesus has given it is what has abiding validity for the members of Matthew's community.

Matthew's twofold concern that, on the one hand, Jesus should not be thought of as an enemy of the Mosaic law but that, on the other, it is his word that supersedes the word of Moses comes to the fore elsewhere in the Gospel. The pericope on divorce and celibacy (19:3–12), for example, reinforces the point of the third antithesis in the Sermon on the Mount (5:31–32): except in the case of the incestuous marriage, divorce is forbidden (19:9; cf. Lev. 18:6–18). In this pericope, too, Matthew pictures Jesus as pitting himself against Moses: "Moses permitted you to divorce your wives . . . but I say to you . . ." (19:8–9). And the fact that Jesus' injunction is indeed radical, even to the point of revoking Mosaic law in order to transcend it, is evident from the disciples' observation and Jesus' reply to them: the disciples assert, "If such is the case of a man with his wife, it is not expedient to marry" (19:10); and Jesus counters, "Not all men can receive this precept . . ." (19:11).

But in other pericopes having to do with the Mosaic law, Matthew portrays Jesus as making his point without at the same time overturning a command of Moses. Thus, in the stories on plucking grain on the sabbath (12:1–8) and on healing the withered hand (12:9–14), Jesus in both instances suppresses the sabbath law in favor of the law of love (12:7, 12). At the same time, he does not declare the sabbath law void (cf. Exod. 20:8–11; Deut. 5:13–14), and the passage 24:20 is indication that Matthew's church observed this law as long as it did not conflict with its ministry of love. In the pericope on clean and unclean (cf. 15:10–20a), Jesus does not, as Mark explains it in his version of the story (cf. 7:19), rescind the dietary laws laid down in Leviticus 11 and Deuteronomy 14. Instead, without at all passing judgment on the question of defilement through outward things such as foods, Jesus in Matthew's account speaks to the issue of the defilement that is of the heart (15:18).

If according to Matthew Jesus upholds the Mosaic law and yet revokes it at points in the interest of more radical precepts, the same can be said of the attitude he takes towards the so-called "tradition of the elders." This tradition, cultivated by Pharisaic Judaism, was oral in form. It consisted of a vast number of regulations, regarded as obligatory for the individual Jew, the purpose of which was to apply the law of Moses to new times and new circumstances. To return to the pericope on clean and unclean (15:1–20), Matthew depicts the Pharisees and scribes as approaching Jesus with the charge that his disciples, because they eat with unwashed hands, are transgressing the tradition of the elders (15:1–2). Later, in private conversation, Jesus tells his disciples that this requirement is not binding on them. "To eat with unwashed hands," he declares flatly, "does not defile a man" (15:20).

In this instance, then, Jesus authoritatively sets aside a stipulated ritual of the tradition of the elders. What is more, in 16:11–12 he warns his disciples to "beware . . . of the teaching of the Pharisees and Sadducees," and in chapter 23 he employs bitter sarcasm in attacking their regulations (cf. also 15:6). On the other hand, in 23:2–3 Matthew describes Jesus as telling the disciples that the "scribes and the Pharisees sit on Moses' seat, so practice and observe whatever they tell you," and in 23:23 Jesus even speaks approvingly of the Pharisaic rule concerning the tithing of "mint and dill and cummin" ("but these things one ought to have done"). On balance, therefore, it seems that the position the church of Matthew takes towards the Pharisaic tradition of the elders is that it complies with it, at least to some undetermined extent, but not if it contravenes the will of God as Jesus has articulated it. The word of Jesus is, again, what is normative for the church.

Although the church of Matthew adheres to the law as Jesus has given it and, to some extent, also to the tradition of the elders, this should not be taken to mean that the mark of its piety is consequently the development of an elaborate system of casuistry. In a number of passages, the Matthaean Jesus makes it eminently clear that the deepest intention of the will of God is love. We have already encountered this in the twin pericopes on plucking grain on the sabbath (cf. 12:7; also 9:13) and on healing the withered hand (cf. 12:12), for in both the sabbath law is suppressed in favor of the law of love. But Matthew furthermore has Jesus state this programmatically: in the so-called "golden rule" in the Sermon on the Mount (7:12), in his statement at 23:23 on the "weightier matters of the law" ("justice," *"mercy,"* and "faithfulness"), and in the pericopes on the rich young man (19:19) and on the great commandment (22:34–40).

To consider the latter unit, Jesus announces that all the law and the prophets hang on two commandments: "You shall love the Lord your God with all your heart, and with all your soul, and with all your mind" (cf. Deut. 6:5); and "You shall love your neighbor as yourself" (cf. Lev. 19:18). As Matthew conceives of these words of Jesus, the idea is not that these commandments are the greatest ones because they are to be valued more highly than the others and hence are to be observed in some sense more diligently.   Instead, the idea is that they reveal the ground, or the intention, of all the precepts of the law or, indeed, of the entire will of God as set forth in the whole of the OT (cf. "law and prophets," 22:40).   That is to say, keeping the injunctions of the law, or doing the will of God, is always, in essence, an exercize in love.   But now we are encroaching upon the discussion of the next section.

The "Greater Righteousness"

Thus far, we have pointed out that through the call of Jesus Messiah, the Son of God, the disciples of Jesus become sons of God and brothers, those who are given to share in his company and so to live in the sphere of God's gracious rule.   As they follow Jesus, he imparts to them, among other things, his teaching.   The content of his teaching is the will of God, so that it is binding on the disciples and on the church for all time to come.   In teaching the will of God, Jesus teaches the law, and in the process intensifies and radicalizes it even to the point where he, the Son, places himself above Moses.   Whether it is a matter of the law or of the so-called tradition of the elders, the word of Jesus, the Messiah Son of God, is consequently what is normative for the disciples and the church.

But how are the disciples to respond to the gracious call of Jesus to follow after him and to the teaching he imparts to them along the way? As Jesus puts it in the Sermon on the Mount and as we mentioned in passing, it is with lives that reflect the "greater righteousness" (5:20). What is the meaning of this concept?

The term "righteousness" (*dikaiosynē*) occurs seven times in the First Gospel, and it appears that Matthew has not appropriated it from the tradition but has himself inserted it in each instance into the gospel materials (cf. 3:15; 5:6, 10, 20; 6:1, 33; 21:32). Basically, Matthew applies it in a twofold manner. Although he alludes to the righteousness of the scribes and Pharisees (5:20), he speaks explicitly of the "righteousness of God" (cf. 6:33; also 5:6) on the one hand and of the "righteousness of the disciples" (cf. 5:20; 6:1; also 5:10) on the other.

The righteousness of God is his justice, which issues in salvation and judgment for humans. Thus, for the disciples of Jesus to "hunger and thirst for righteousness" (5:6) is for them to long fervently for God to establish his just rule over all the world, a longing that, Jesus pledges, will be satisfied. Similarly, the injunction to "seek first the kingdom and his [the Father's] righteousness" (6:33) is a summons to the disciples to orient their lives towards the approaching, consummated Rule of God and the end-time salvation attendant to it. Jesus exhorts the disciples to pray for this themselves in the second and third petitions of the Lord's Prayer: ". . . thy kingdom come, thy will be done, on earth as it is in heaven" (6:10).

But Matthew also predicates "righteousness" to the disciples ("your righteousness"). In this connection, the term denotes doing the will of God, the heavenly Father (7:21; 12:50; 18:14; 21:31a), or, to use a metaphor, "producing fruit" (cf. 7:16–20; 12:33; 13:23; 21:43). For the disciples, for example, to be "persecuted on account of righteousness" (5:10) is for them to be persecuted because they lead lives pleasing to God and consonant with being in the sphere of his rule. And for them to "beware of practicing their [your] righteousness before men" (6:1) is for them to be on their guard lest they be hypocritical (6:2, 5, 16) in their piety or the conduct of their lives.

Against this background, we return to the key passage 5:20. Here the Matthaean Jesus tells the disciples that "unless your righteousness exceeds that of the scribes and Pharisees, you will never enter the kingdom of heaven." As is obvious, the meaning of the term "righteousness" in this verse is likewise that of doing the will of God: the piety of the disciples is to be superior to that of the scribes and Pharisees. What does Matthew have in mind in recording this saying of Jesus?

Negatively, the point of comparing the piety of the disciples with that of the scribes and Pharisees has to do with the circumstance that Matthew pictures Jesus elsewhere in the Gospel as charging the leaders of Israel with "hypocrisy" (cf. esp. 23:28; also 23:13, 15–16, 23, 25, 27, 29). Now Jesus defines hypocrisy as saying one thing and doing another (23:3). But such duplicity is by no means a relatively small matter of little consequence. On the contrary, it is indicative of "lawlessness" (*anomia*), of not doing the will of God and therefore of producing "rotten fruit" that will result in condemnation to Gehenna (3:7–10; 12:33–37; 23:13, 15, 27–28, 33). In view of this, we recognize that the adjective "greater" in the expression the "greater righteousness" must be pressed beyond the normal signification of the word: in reality, the righteousness that Jesus requires of the disciples in 5:20 is not simply different in degree from that of the scribes and Pharisees but, indeed, different in kind.

What the expression the "greater righteousness" signifies positively Matthew explains in the pivotal passage 5:48. This is the verse with which he concludes the entire section of the Sermon on the Mount devoted to the antitheses. In 5:48, the Matthaean Jesus exhorts the disciples: "You, therefore, shall be *perfect* (*teleioi*), as your heavenly Father is perfect." Deut. 18:13 shows how the first half of this saying is to be understood: "You shall be *whole-hearted* [LXX: *teleios* ("perfect")] in the service of the Lord your God" (NEB). In line with this, the righteousness of the disciples is to be "greater" in the sense that they are to be absolutely single-hearted, or undivided ("whole," "complete"), in their doing of the will of God.

Matthew uses the adjective "perfect" one other time in his Gospel (19:21), in the story of the rich young man (19:16–22). This story alerts us once again to the proper context within which Matthew treats of the "greater righteousness." As Matthew tells it, the young man, desirous of obtaining eternal life, affirms to Jesus that he has observed all the commandments, and asks him whether there is anything he still lacks (19:16–20). In reply, Jesus remarks: "If you would be perfect [whole, complete], go, sell what you possess and give to the poor, and you will have treasure in heaven; and come, follow me" (19:21). The critical point in these words is that perfection ("wholeness," "completeness"), the reward of which is eternal life, is associated with following after Jesus. Hence, for Matthew, the proper context for doing the greater righteousness, for observing the will of God, is, quite singularly, discipleship.

Accordingly, Matthew defines the greater righteousness as doing the will of God, and he firmly associates it with discipleship. But what is the hallmark of the greater righteousness, of doing the will of God? The hallmark is, of course, love: love towards God, and love towards the neighbor (19:18–19; 22:37–39). Towards God, the disciples assume the posture of "little ones," that is, they humble themselves before God and depend upon him totally (18:3–4, 6, 10), and they do the will of God as Jesus has taught it (cf. 5:2–7:29). Towards the neighbor, the disciples are the "servants" of all and not the "lords" of all (20:25–26), the "slaves" of all and not the "bosses" ("first") of all (20:27).

In their exercise of the greater righteousness, the disciples are not without example. In fact, Matthew places them in the long train of all those in the history of salvation held to be "the righteous" (*dikaioi*). Cases in point in the time of Israel (OT) are Abel (23:35), the prophets (5:10–12), the saints (13:17; 23:29), and the martyrs (23:35). In the time of Jesus (earthly—exalted), they are such as Joseph (1:19), John the Baptist (21:32), and Christian missionaries (10:41). But the foremost example is Jesus himself.

In one of the scenes of Jesus' trial before Pilate, Matthew terms Jesus in the words of Pilate's wife "that righteous man" (27:19), and by this he intends to show that Jesus is completely innocent of any wrongdoing (cf. 27:4, 24). Still, this scene merely underlines the circumstance that, in Matthew's eyes, Jesus is the one par excellence who does the will of God. This comes to the fore already in the story of the baptism (3:13–17), where Jesus, in the first words he utters in the Gospel, indicates that he submits to baptism by John, not out of need for repentance and the confession of sins as is the case with Israel (3:2, 5–6, 11), but because this, too, is in accordance with the will of God (3:15). Other pericopes in the Gospel that likewise portray Jesus in a special way as the one who is perfectly obedient to the will of God are the stories of the temptation (4:1–11), of Jesus in Gethsemane (26:39, 42), and of Jesus on the cross (27:39–44). Furthermore, it is as one who himself does the will of God perfectly that Jesus also bids his disciples to pray to God, ". . . thy will be done, on earth as it is in heaven" (6:10), or announces to them that his true relatives are those who do the "will of my Father who is in heaven" (12:50), or warns them that the only ones who will ever enter the kingdom of heaven are, again, those who do the "will of my Father who is in heaven" (7:21; cf. also 18:14).

Consequently, Matthew does indeed regard Jesus Messiah, the Son of God, as the "righteous one" par excellence. As such, he is the preeminent "model" for the disciples and church of what it is to do the greater righteousness. But true as this is, it is just as true that Matthew never permits this facet of his portrait of Jesus to blur or to diminish in the slightest his uniqueness. Although the followers of Jesus are to emulate him, there is no thought in Matthew's conception of things that they can ever become his equals. The Sonship and the obedience to the will of God which Matthew predicates to Jesus Messiah, he predicates to no one else.

One further matter begs for consideration. Matthew places the disciples and therefore also the members of his church in line with all "the righteous" in the history of salvation, and the exhortation they receive is that they are to do the "greater righteousness." At the same time, except for what appears to be post-Easter Christian missionaries who seem to have run the high risk of martyrdom (cf. 10:40–41 to 23:34–35), followers of Jesus are never designated in the First Gospel as "the righteous." Instead, Matthew, as we shall observe next section, reserves the predication "the righteous" for those of his contemporaries only whom the Son of Man will declare at the Last Judgment to have, in truth, done the will of God (cf. 13:43, 49; 25:37, 46).

The Church of Matthew

It is clear from the preceding discussion that Matthew's portrait of the church is not without its exalted features. Through the gracious summons of Jesus Messiah, the Son of God, the disciples of Jesus become sons of God and brothers, and enter into the sphere of God's kingly rule. In response to this gracious summons, the disciples reflect in their lives the greater righteousness, which is to say that they do the will of God as Jesus makes it known. In terms of Matthew's "kingdom language," it may be said of the church that here are "sons of the kingdom" (5:9, 45; 13:38) to whom God has "given the kingdom" (21:43), who in Jesus Son of God share the "forgiveness" of the kingdom (1:21; 26:28; 27:38–54) and hear and understand the "word of the kingdom" (13:19, 23), who have been "instructed about the kingdom" (13:52) and hence know the "secrets of the kingdom" (13:11), who seek the "righteousness of the kingdom" (6:33) and have been entrusted with the "keys of the kingdom" (16:19), who pray fervently for the "coming of the kingdom" (6:10) and produce the "fruits of the kingdom" (13:8, 23; 21:43), and who at the consummation of the age will "enter the kingdom" (cf. 25:21, 23) and "inherit" it (5:3, 10; 25:34).

But despite this exalted view of the church, it is noteworthy that Matthew steadfastly refuses to identify the church with the kingdom of heaven. Instead, he associates it with the kingdom. One reason why Matthew associates, but does not identify, the church with the kingdom surely has to do with the circumstance that it is by no stretch of the imagination a pure community of the holy. On the contrary, it is a *corpus mixtum* ("mixed [disunited] body"), and one indication of this is the fact that while Matthew attributes to its members the status of being "the called" (22:14), he noticeably reserves the status of being "the elect" (22:14; 24:22, 24, 31) or, as we saw, "the righteous" (13:43, 49; 25:37, 46; but cf. 10:41) for those members only to whom the Son of man will grant at the latter day "eternal life" (25:46).

In the present age, the church is caught up in the throes of the so-called messianic woes (24:8). Not only does it suffer persecution at the hands of Jews (5:11–12; 10:17, 23; 13:21; 23:34) and tribulation at the hands of gentiles (13:21; 24:9), but it is also afflicted by internal difficulties, such as the following: there are members who do "not understand" the Word of the kingdom and consequently are without true faith (13:19), or who are "false prophets" and lead other disciples astray (7:15–23; 24:11), or who surrender their faith because they cannot endure persecution or tribulation (13:21; 24:9–10), or whose lives as disciples remain sterile because their faith succumbs to the cares of the world or to the seduction of wealth (13:22), or who deny Jesus Son of God (10:33), or who despise others in the community (18:10), or betray fellow-disciples to gentile opponents (24:10), or cause other disciples to lose their faith (18:6). And there is the threat of status-seeking in the church (23:8–12), hatred among members (24:10), rampant "lawlessness" resulting in lovelessness (24:12; cf. 20:15), lukewarmness towards Christian duty (25:26), an unwillingness to forgive the neighbor (18:35), and other evil that threatens the spiritual welfare of the community (cf. 15:19).

In response to this situation in which he at once affirms the presence of God's rule in his community but must catalogue its many aberrations from the will of God, Matthew directs the attention of his church squarely to the consummation of the age (*synteleia tou aiōnos*) and the inauguration of the future kingdom by Jesus Son of man (cf. 10:23; 13:30, 39b–43, 49–50; 16 27–28; 19:28–29; 24:3, 27, 39, 42, 44; 25:31–46). He does this in order that his community might see the present as decisively qualified by the future and recognize that the disciple pursues life only in the light of the approaching kingdom. The fact of the matter is that the God who will miraculously establish his rule "then" is even "now" at work in his Son to motivate the disciple ethically to do his will. Throughout this age, therefore, what characterizes the life of the disciple and of the church in their relation to the kingdom of heaven is this tension between present and future, which is at the same time a tension between "ethics" and "eschatology" (cf., e.g., 5:3–10, 19–20; 6:33; 7:21; 12:40; 13:40–41; 17:9; 24:27, 37, 38–39).

In application of this "ethical-eschatological tension" to the life of the church, Matthew both warns and exhorts his fellow-members. Negatively, he sternly reminds them that the possession of wealth poses the most serious kind of threat to the disciple who would "enter" the future kingdom (19:23), that those who cause another disciple to lose his faith or who forfeit their own will be severely punished (18:6, 8–9), that the coming of Jesus Son of man for judgment will catch unawares those who are not prepared for it (24:36–39, 40–42, 43–44, 50–51; 25:11–13, 24–30), that those who do not do the will of God in the present can be certain that their appeals to the Son of man at the latter day will avail them nothing (7:15–23), and that in this present age they dare never forget that the church, too, will most assuredly undergo judgment at the consummation (13:47–50; 24:45–51; 25:1–13, 14–30).

Positively, Matthew exhorts the members of his community to all of the following: to see their lives in the present as being shaped by God's future promises (5:3–10); to be diligent in offering their (eschatological) petitions to God, especially the prayer Jesus taught them (6:9–13); to practice a piety that is pleasing to God against that day when he will bestow upon them his eschatological "reward" (cf. 5:12; 6:4, 6, 18; 10:41–42); to emulate in the present the Lord Jesus, Son of God, so that each one "takes up his cross and follows" him, thus "finding" his life even while "losing" it (10:24–25, 38–39; 16:24–26); to have no fear of their enemies but to commend themselves to the providential care of the God who can condemn to Gehenna (10:28–31) and to depend upon him as completely as does a child his father (18:3–4); to suffer persecution with joy as ones who will inherit the kingdom (5:10–12); and to be like faithful slaves (24:45; 25:21, 23) who are totally committed to the doing of the will of God (6:10, 33; 13:44, 45–46), being ever watchful and ready in view of the unexpected coming of Jesus Son of man (24:27, 32–35, 45–46; 25:10, 20–23).

In sum, as Matthew understands it, the church of Jesus, the exalted Son of God, is the eschatological people of God whose existence is characterized by a tension between the present and the future. Even now the church lives in the sphere of the gracious rule of God as exercised by Jesus and has as its commission to proclaim the gospel of the kingdom to the nations and hence to invite them, too, to enter this sphere. But though the church lives under God's rule, it is in no wise immune to the forces of evil. On the contrary, it is exposed in the present to the so-called messianic woes. Severely afflicted as it is from within and without, Matthew calls the church to see its present situation in the light of the future kingdom of heaven. In this way, the members of the community, through eschatological warning and exhortation, are brought face to face in the present with the God of the future kingdom who would, through his Son, motivate them ethically to do his will and so be heirs of life.

The Situation of Matthew

Scholars generally associate Matthew's Gospel with the city of Antioch in Syria. As to date, they place it at about A.D. 85 or 90, reasoning that it was written some fifteen or twenty years following the destruction of Jerusalem, alluded to in 22:7, and the writing of Mark, which Matthew apparently used. To turn from the theological portrait Matthew sketches of Jesus and of the disciples, our final task is to ask as to the kind of community that stands behind the First Gospel. What can be said about it as a sociological entity?

The language the Matthaean community speaks is almost certainly Greek. This is indicated already by the quality of the language of the First Gospel. It is not what may be termed "translation Greek," the secondary rendering, for example, of a Hebrew or Aramaic original. Seemingly, Matthew has placed Mark, itself written in Greek, at the basis of his Gospel, and the so-called document Q has also come to him in Greek form. In a test of the language of the First Gospel, C. F. D. Moule states that although Matthew betrays a feeling for "Semitic atmosphere" and has at times taken over Semitisms from his sources or even given a phrase a Semitic twist himself (cf., e.g., 7:28; 11:1; 13:53; 19:1; 26:1: *"And it happened* when Jesus finished . . ."), he can be seen on the whole to have been "an educated person commanding sound Greek with a considerable vocabulary."[30]

If we judge from the contents of the Gospel, the members of the Matthaean community are of both Jewish and gentile background. Features of the Gospel that suggest that Matthew has written for a sizeable Jewish-Christian constituency are numerous. For one thing, Matthew utilizes key terms that are Jewish in tone. The sanctified life of the disciple, for example, is known as "righteousness" (*dikaiosynē;* cf., e.g., 5:20; 6:1). The preferred designation for the rule of God is "the kingdom of heaven" instead of "the kingdom of God," which is the expression Mark and Luke employ. God is often referred to as "your heavenly Father" or as "your Father who is in heaven" (cf. the Sermon on the Mount) and the disciples of Jesus as "sons of God" (5:9), "sons of your Father who is in heaven" (5:45), or "sons of the kingdom" (13:38). The end of time and the final day are termed, respectively, "the consummation of the age" (cf., e.g., 13:39, 40, 49) and "the day of judgment" (cf. 11:22, 24; 12:36). These are but a sampling of Matthew's penchant for "Jewish-like" phraseology.

The Matthaean picture of Jesus is likewise Jewish in hue. He is the "Son of Abraham," the one in whom the entire history of Israel reaches its culmination (1:1–17). He is furthermore the "Messiah" (cf. 1:1, 16, 17, 18), or "Coming One" (cf. 11:2–3), who has been sent specifically to the "lost sheep from the house of Israel" (15:24). He is also the "Son of David," the royal figure who stands in the line of David (1:1, 6, 17, 20, 25; 21:5, 9), the "King of Israel [the Jews]" who suffers on behalf of his people (chap. 27). Indeed, Jesus is, in sum, the "Son of God," or "Emmanuel," the eschatological "Shepherd" in whom God, in fulfillment of OT prophecy, has drawn near to dwell with his people to the end of the age (1:23; 2:6, 15; 18:20; 28:20) and who will, as the "Son of man," return to judge all humankind (25:31–46).

The ministry of Jesus, too, has a particularly Jewish aura about it in the First Gospel. Matthew is at pains to show that it takes place almost exclusively within the confines ot Israel (cf. 15:24; also 10:6). Except for his fateful journey to Jerusalem (cf. 19:1), Galilee is the place of Jesus' activity (4:12, 18, 23), especially the environs of Capernaum (cf chaps. 8–9; 11:23; 17:24), which is "his own city" (9:1) where he "dwells" (4:13) and may have a "house" (cf. 9:10, 28; 12:46 and 13:1; 13:36; 17:25). Thus, it is *from* Galilee that the news of Jesus spreads throughout all Syria (4:24), and it is *to* Galilee that the crowds from the Decapolis, Jerusalem, Judea, and across the Jordan come to be with him (4:25). When Jesus leaves Galilee, it is only briefly (cf., e.g., 3:13–4:13; 8:23–9:1; 16:13–20 [but cf. 17:22]). In fact, on one occasion when he withdraws into the regions of Tyre and Sidon, it appears that he merely crosses the border, for it is said of the Canaanite woman that she "came out" towards Jesus (15:21–28).

Until Easter, the disciples in the First Gospel also share in Jesus' concentration on Israel. Matthew devotes the whole of the section 9:35–10:42 to their projected mission to Israel, which goes beyond anything one finds in either Mark or Luke.

The attitude Jesus takes towards the law and the tradition of the elders is yet another factor that suggests that Matthew has written for a strong Jewish-Christian constituency. Although Matthew, as we saw, depicts Jesus as abrogating at points both the law and the tradition of the elders (cf., e.g., 5:31–32, 33–37, 38–42; 19:3–12; 15:20), he also depicts him as upholding both to the extent that they do not conflict with his teaching of the will of God (cf. 5:17–18; 24:20; 23:2–3, 23). The Marcan Jesus, by contrast, appears to overthrow the legal system of the Jews (cf. 7:1–23).

Finally, the manner in which Matthew treats certain other details argues for the Jewishness of a large segment of his community. Unlike Mark, Matthew does not, for instance, explain such Jewish regulations as the washing of the hands before meals (cf. 15:2 with Mark 7:2–4), and neither does he explain the custom of wearing amulets and tassels (23:5). Semitic words, while translated at times (cf. "Emmanuel," 1:23; "Golgotha," 27:33; cry of dereliction, 27:46) are at other times left untranslated (cf. *"hraka,"* 5:22; *"Beelzeboul,"* 10:25; *"korbanan,"* 27:6), and it is furthermore assumed that the readers will be familiar with a peculiarly Jewish turn of phrase (cf., e.g., "straining out the gnat," 23:24; "whitewashed tombs," 23:27).

But if the unmistakable Jewishness of much of the First Gospel favors the thesis that Matthew has written it with a sizeable Jewish-Christian constituency in mind, the attitude he takes towards the mission to the nations shows that there are also Christians in his community of gentile origin. One looks in vain in the First Gospel for traces of the fierce controversy surrounding the gentile mission which are so prominent in Paul (cf. Galatians 2) and Acts (chap. 15). On the contrary, one can detect in the First Gospel from beginning to end a pronounced "gentile bias." Already in the genealogy of Jesus, four non-Israelite women are listed as the ancestors of Jesus ("Tamar," "Rahab," "Ruth," and "the wife of Uriah" [Bathsheba], 1:3, 5–6). In chapter 2, the "Magi from the East" are described as "worshiping" Jesus and presenting him gifts (vv. 1–2, 11). Jesus' settling in "Galilee of the gentiles" to begin his ministry to Israel prefigures the post-Easter return of the disciples to Galilee, from where they will undertake their mission to the nations (4:12, 15; 28:7, 16–20; cf. also 10:18). As the second of a series of ten miracles, Jesus heals the servant of a centurion, and attendant to this he declares: "Truly, I say to you, not even in Israel have I found such faith; I tell you, many will come from east and west and sit at table with Abraham, Isaac, and Jacob in the kingdom of heaven" (8:5–13). At 12:21, Matthew quotes from the OT in order to proclaim Jesus as the one in whom the "gentiles will hope," and at 13:38 he writes that it is in the "world" that "sons of the kingdom" will be raised up. In the parables of the wicked husbandmen (21:33–46) and of the great supper (22:1–14), Matthew employs figurative speech to depict the influx of the gentiles into the church (cf. 21:41; 22:9–10), and, more directly, he has Jesus announce in 24:14 and 26:13 that it is throughout the entire world that the gospel of the kingdom will be proclaimed. Last, the circumstance that Matthew in a saying of Jesus can also designate the church as a "nation" (21:43) further goes to prove that his community has in fact surmounted the problem of the mission to the nations and that increasingly gentiles are joining its ranks.

A church with members of Jewish and gentile origin, the Matthaean community is "urban" and prosperous as well. In comparison with Mark, who uses the word "city" (*polis*) eight times and the word "village" (*kōmē*) seven times, Matthew uses the word "village" only four times but the word "city" no fewer than twenty-six times. The latter statistic is all the more striking when it is observed that several occurrences of the word "city" seem to relate to circumstances in Matthew's own time (cf. 10:11, 14, 15, 23; 23:34; also 5:14). Perhaps, then, the Matthaean church is a "city church."[31]

The evidence that this church is also well-to-do is strong. The Lucan Jesus, for example, pronounces a blessing on "the poor" (6:20), but the Matthaean Jesus pronounces a blessing on "the poor in spirit" (5:3). The Marcan Jesus commands the disciples in conjunction with their missionary journey to take with them no "copper coin," that is, small change (6:8), but the Matthaean Jesus commands them to take no "gold, nor silver, nor copper coin" (10:9). The Lucan Jesus tells a parable about "minas" (19:11–27), but the Matthaean Jesus tells a parable about "talents" (25:14–30), one of the latter being worth approximately fifty times as much as one of the former. The Lucan Jesus says in the words of the householder in the parable of the great supper: "Go out quickly to the streets and lanes of the city, and bring in the poor and maimed and blind and lame" (14:21); but the Matthaean Jesus simply says in his version of these words: "Go therefore to the thoroughfares, and invite to the marriage feast as many as you find" (22:9). In Mark (15:43) and Luke (23:50–51), Joseph of Arimathea is a member of the council who is looking for the kingdom of God, but in Matthew he is a "rich man . . . who also was a disciple of Jesus" (27:57).

It seems, in fact, that the community behind the First Gospel is well accustomed to dealing in a wide range of money. Whereas Luke mentions "silver" and a few kinds of money (cf., e.g., 7:41; 12:6,

59; 19:13) and Mark mentions an assortment of what on the whole were the lesser denominations, Matthew makes no reference whatever to the *lepton*, the smallest unit of money cited in the Gospels (a small copper coin = c. $\frac{1}{8}¢$), but does refer to all of the following: the *kodrantēs* ("quadrans" = c. $\frac{1}{4}¢$), the *assarion* ("assarion" = c. 1¢) the *dēnarion* ("denarius" = c. 18¢), the *didrachmon* ("double drachma" = c. 36¢), the *statēr* ("stater" = c. 80¢), the *talanton* ("talent" = c. $1080), and to *chalkos* ("copper coin"), *argyrion* ("silver"), *argyros* ("silver"), and *chrysos* ("gold"). Indeed, if we take the three terms "silver," "gold," and "talent," we discover that they occur in the First Gospel no fewer than twenty-eight times, which may be compared with the single use of the word "silver" by Mark and the fourfold use of it by Luke. Against a background of wealth such as these terms indicate, it makes sense that Matthew should appropriate Mark's warning against riches in 13:22 (Mark 4:19) and sharpen the saying of Jesus at 19:23 so that difficulty in entering the kingdom is predicated, not merely to "those who have means" (Mark 10:23), but to the "rich man." In light of the preceding, it looks, again, as though the Matthaean community is in no sense materially disadvantaged.

Accordingly, from what we can tell the church of Matthew, firmly established by the last decades of the first century, is a Greek-speaking community of people of Jewish and gentile origin which is rather well-to-do and situated in or near a city, most likely Antioch in Syria. Now it furthermore seems, as we noted above in passing, that the social and religious climate in which this community finds itself is one of intense conflict. On the one hand, it appears that these Christians are living in close proximity to hostile pagans. Whether or not their mission to the nations is the sole reason, Matthew speaks of them as being hauled into court by gentile authorities, judicially harassed ("handed over to tribulation"), hated "by all," and even put to death (10:18, 22; 13:21; 24:9). Clearly, Matthew depicts members of his church as enduring persecution from the side of their gentile neighbors.[32]

But it likewise appears that the Matthaean church is living in close proximity to a vigorous Jewish community. The evidence for this is multiple. For instance, the parable of the tares (13:24–30) may refer to this directly, for it is possibly in regard to the church's relationship to Israel that Matthew reports Jesus as saying, "Let both grow side by side until the harvest" (13:30).[33] In a similar vein, if the story of the payment of the temple tax (17:24–27) can be interpreted to mean that the Jewish Christians in Matthew's community are being encouraged, despite their "freedom," not to offend Jews by refusing to participate in the collection of contributions throughout Jewry in support of the Patriarchy at Jamnia,[34] then this unit, too, may speak for close contact between Jews and the church of Matthew.

Perhaps Matthew's presentation of Jesus, of the disciples, and of the leaders of the Jews also gives indication that the Matthaean church lives in close proximity to Jews. Thus, it may secondarily be with an eye to the Jews about him that Matthew has portrayed Jesus Son of God as the ideal Israelite (cf., e.g., 4:1–11) and has elevated him above Moses as the supreme teacher of the will of God (cf. the Sermon on the Mount). In addition, Matthew's description of Christian piety as the righteousness that is "greater" than that of the scribes and Pharisees may also have the Jews "next door" in mind (5:20), and this could further be the case for the many invectives that are hurled at the Jewish leaders throughout the Gospel (cf. chap. 23). On another level, although the essential task of the church in the time of Matthew is unquestionably to make disciples of the nations (28:18–20), this does not mean, as we mentioned earlier, that no missionary activity whatever is being done among Jews. The missionary discourse of chapter 10, which has to do with evangelization especially among Jews but also among gentiles (cf. vv. 17–18, 22–23), is not without relevance for the church of Matthew, and the passage 23:34 is an unmistakable reference to missionary activity among the Jews which, seemingly, is taking place in Matthew's day. The church's mission to the Jews has not met with success and its task henceforth is to go to the gentiles, but continued work among the Jews points to no lack of interaction between Matthew's church and the Jewish community.

Still, if Matthew's church lives in close proximity to a strong Jewish community, it is not to be thought of as a "splinter group" that is nevertheless a member of the Jewish league of synagogues.[35] The place of Matthew's church is no longer within Judaism but without it. Several factors compel this conclusion.

To begin with, Matthew more rigorously than either Mark or Luke, makes of Jesus and his disciples a group set apart from the Israelite crowds and their leaders. This comes to the fore already in the way in which Matthew has persons address Jesus and develops his ecclesiological concept of "being with Jesus." As for the latter, we observed at the outset of this chapter that Matthew very carefully reserves for the disciples alone the privilege of sharing in the company, or presence, of Jesus, so that it is not said of Judas or of the crowds or of the Israelite leaders that they are "with Jesus" or he "with them." Correlatively, Matthew distinguishes sharply, as we have also seen, between the manner in which the disciples and persons without faith approach Jesus: whereas the disciples address him as "Lord," opponents and persons without faith address him only as "rabbi" or "teacher." The "apartness" of Jesus and his disciples in the First Gospel reflects, we believe, the religious distance that separates the Matthaean church from the Jewish community.

Matthew's use of the expression "their [your] synagogue(s)," his massive apology against Israel as an institution, and the organizational autonomy of his community are further indications that his church has already broken with Judaism. To take the last point first, Matthew's community, as we shall learn in a moment, is not at all under Jewish religious control but has its own form of organization that deals with such weighty matters as those of doctrine and of church order. In addition, by regularly appending the modifying genitive "your" or "their" to the noun "synagogue(s)" (cf. 4:23; 9:35; 10:17; 12:9; 13:54; 23:34), Matthew attests idiomatically to the disassociation of his community from Judaism. Also, except to acknowledge that the "scribes and the Pharisees are seated on the chair of Moses" (23:2), Matthew has virtually nothing good to say of Israel as a religious institution. Typically, there is no "friendly scribe" in the first Gospel as there is in the Second of whom it is written: "And when Jesus saw that he answered wisely, he said to him, 'You are not far from the kingdom of God' " (Mark 12:34). On the contrary, the one scribe in the First Gospel who requests of Jesus that he become his disciple is flatly refused with the words: "Foxes have holes, and the birds of the air nests, but the Son of man has nowhere to lay his head" (8:20).[36] Indeed, far from evincing affinity for contemporary Israel, Matthew, as we saw last chapter, mounts a massive apology against it. As far as he is concerned, contemporary Israel is, as a saying of Jesus puts it, a "plant which my heavenly Father has not planted [and] will be rooted up" (15:13). And if persecution characterizes the relationship of Matthew's church with the gentiles, this is all the more the case, we know, with contemporary Israel (cf. 5:10–12; 10:17, 23, 28; 23:34–35).

Consequently, the Matthaean community, a church with members of Jewish and gentile background which stands outside the orbit of official Judaism but lives in close proximity to both Jews and gentiles, encounters from without persecution on the part of both Jew and gentile. What is to be said of the internal structure of the community?

Called through baptism to follow Jesus, the risen and exalted Son of God who presides over and resides in his church (28:19–20; also 1:23; 18:20), the Christians of Matthew's community know themselves to be "sons of God" (5:9, 45; 13:38) and "brothers" of Jesus and of one another (12:49–50; 18:35; 23:8; 25:40; 28:10). As sons of God, they are also the "little ones," for they recognize that they are totally dependent upon their heavenly Father (18:3, 6, 10). As the brothers of Jesus and of one another, they are at the same time the "servants" and the "slaves" of one another (20:25–28). And as the followers of Jesus, they are likewise "disciples" (*mathētai*; cf., e.g., 8:23), for they have taken upon themselves his yoke and they "learn" from him (11:29; cf. also 10:24–25). Internally, therefore, the Matthaean community may be described as a brotherhood of the sons of God and the disciples of Jesus.

Within this brotherhood, two or three groups can be distinguished. The one group is that of the "prophets" (10:41; 23:34). In principle, Matthew regards his entire community as standing in the tradition of the OT prophets and the twelve disciples of Jesus (5:12; 13:17). It appears, however, that there are also Christians in his own time who are specifically thought of as "prophets." They are described as itinerant missionaries who proclaim the gospel of the kingdom to Jews (cf. 10:41 to 10:6, 17, 23; 23:34 to 23:29a) but especially to gentiles (cf. 10:41 to 10:18; 24:14; 26:13; 28:19).

Whether these Christian prophets function exclusively beyond the Matthaean community is difficult to say. In 7:15–23, Matthew makes reference to prophets who plainly are active within his com-

munity.   At the same time, he denounces them as "false," as "raven-
ous wolves . . . who come to you in sheep's clothing" (7:15).   What
is more, they are enthusiasts, for it is said that in the name of Christ
they prophesy, cast out demons, and perform many miracles (7:22).
Their works, however, are castigated as contravening their profes-
sion of the name of Christ (7:16–20).   The result is that Matthew
condemns them in words of Jesus as "workers of lawlessness" whom
the Son of man at the latter day will banish from his presence (7:23).
The point is, is one to infer from Matthew's reference to these false
prophets who are at work within his community and against whom he
polemicizes so vigorously that, conversely, the legitimate Christian
prophets, too, are to be thought of as carrying out a ministry not only
as missionaries beyond the community but also as preachers of the
gospel of the kingdom within the community?   One can only conjec-
ture.

We have identified one or possibly two groups within the Matthaean community: the "prophets" and the "false prophets."   Another identifiable group is those who function as teachers.   They are
designated variously.   Thus, the term "righteous man" (dikaios,
10:41) denotes a teacher of righteousness,[37] and the terms "rabbi"
(hrabbi, 23:8), "scribe" (grammateus, 23:34), and "wise man"
(sophos, 23:34) most likely refer without distinction to those who
are expert in matters pertaining to the Scriptures and the law.[38]   The
verses 10:41 and 23:34, in which three of these four terms occur,
show that Christian teachers, too, serve as missionaries to the Jews,
perhaps conversing or debating with them about the meaning of the
Scriptures, the law, and the traditions in the light of the coming of
Jesus Messiah.

But these Christians who serve as teachers are likewise active
within the community, as can be presupposed from the passage
23:8–12 (cf. also 13:52).   What their exact competences are is
hard to know.   Still, at one point this question becomes acute, because it touches on the matter of the regulation of the life of the
community.

Now Matthew's church has developed a structure for governing
communal life.   In 16:19, for example, Peter receives from Jesus
promise of the power of the "keys of the kingdom of heaven."   He
receives this promise, however, in his capacity as the "first" of the

disciples to be called (4:18–20; 10:2; 16:16) and therefore as the one who is their "spokesman" and who is "typical" of them and of later Christians.[39] Peter's "primacy," therefore, is not that of being elevated to a station above the other disciples but is "salvation-historical" in nature: he is, again, the "first" disciple whom Jesus called to follow him. Since Peter is the first among the disciples all of whom have been called and are in this sense equal, the power of the keys Jesus promises him is perhaps best equated with the power of "binding and loosing," which the other disciples exercise as well as he (cf. 16:19 to 18:18). The power of "binding and loosing," in turn, pertains to the regulation of church doctrine and discipline.[40] Accordingly, whatever the particular contribution of those who serve as teachers, it is the entire Matthaean community that decides the matters of doctrine and discipline. As the passage 18:18 20 indicates, this community makes such decisions gathered together in the name and hence in the presence and on the authority of the exalted Son of God. Moreover, as it does so, it is conscious of the fact that the touchstone of whatever it decides is that it must be in keeping with the injunction given by Jesus to "observe all that I have commanded you" (28:20).

The Matthaean community, then, is without a peculiar "teaching office" such as contemporary Judaism is in the process of developing. Indeed, with an eye towards those engaged in teaching, Matthew is explicit about the problem of position and status. This is reflected by the circumstance that the Matthaean Jesus expressly forbids them to arrogate to themselves a station that would set them above the rest of the community. They are not, for example, to assume the title of "rabbi" or "teacher" (*didaskalos, kathēgētēs*), for these titles are the prerogative of Jesus Messiah, the Son of God (23:8, 10). Neither are they to assume the title of "Father," for this title is the prerogative of God himself (23:9). They are to be the opposite of the "scribes and Pharisees" in contemporary Judaism, who have office and authority but "shut the kingdom of heaven against men," neither entering themselves nor allowing those who would enter to go in (23:13). On the contrary, in the church "all . . . are brothers" (23:8), and the eschatological maxim applies that "whoever exalts himself will be humbled, and whoever humbles himself will be exalted" (23:12).

A word is in order about Matthew himself, the author of the First Gospel. In greatest measure, scholarly opinion does not identify Matthew the author with Matthew the apostle. One reason is that if Matthew is dependent upon Mark, as most scholars believe, it is difficult to explain how it could happen that the apostle Matthew, an eyewitness of the ministry of Jesus, should have taken the greater part of his Gospel from Mark, whom no one claims was a disciple or eyewitness of Jesus. Another reason is that the theological outlook of the writer of the Gospel seems to be that of the second, not the first, generation of Christians to follow Jesus. One might also ask, if it is correct that the Gospel was written about A.D. 85 or 90, whether the apostle Matthew could reasonably be expected to have lived long enough to write this book.

It could be, however, that the apostle Matthew, although not the author of the First Gospel, was associated at one time with the church that stands behind it, and was esteemed as a founder or "patron disciple." This would explain why the story of the call of Matthew (9:9) substitutes in the First Gospel for the story of the call of Levi (cf. Mark 2:14; Luke 5:27), and why the list of the disciples of Jesus has been adjusted accordingly (cf. 10:3 ["Matthew the tax collector"] with Mark 6:18 and Luke 9:15).

Still, some scholars, while they agree that Matthew the apostle did not write the First Gospel, nevertheless hold that his association with it was more direct than this. Appealing to a notice of the second-century church father Papias, which reads that "Matthew wrote [collected] the oracles [accounts] in the Hebrew language and every one interpreted them as he was able,"[41] they contend that Matthew the apostle was the author of a primitive Aramaic document that was subsequently taken up into the First Gospel. In its various forms, this thesis has been thoroughly debated over the years, but the results have been inconclusive.

Can, then, Matthew the author be identified? The answer is no. It is sometimes suggested that the First Gospel was produced, not by an individual, but by a school.[42] Most scholars, however, prefer to think in terms of individual authorship. A few argue that the Gospel was written by a gentile Christian, basing their case on the author's alleged "distance" from Judaism, on his use of the LXX and treatment of certain Semitic words and other terms, and on the supposed relationship within the Gospel between tradition (= Jewish Christian) and redaction (= gentile Christian).[43]   But by far the majority of scholars regard the author as a Christian of Jewish background, and they point to many of his theological emphases and to the architechtonic structure of his work as proof that he had enjoyed rabbinical training.   Perhaps, therefore, Matthew the author can best be described as a Greek-speaking Jewish Christian of the second generation after Christ who possessed a universal missionary outlook and had most probably enjoyed rabbinical training.

To conclude, the church of Matthew, by the last two decades of the first century A.D., must be regarded as a firmly established community.   Greek is its language, and the constituency is of both Jewish and gentile origin.   It is furthermore "urban" and well to-do, located perhaps in or near Syrian Antioch, and its neighbors are Jews and gentiles.   The atmosphere in which it lives is one of conflict, both from within and from without.   From without, it encounters gentile but especially Jewish persecution.   From within, it is troubled by miracle-working false prophets, among others.   Still, this community, having had its ties with contemporary Judaism severed, conceives of itself as the brotherhood of the sons of God and of the disciples of Jesus.   It knows the exalted Son of God to reside in its midst, and it traces its teaching and ethics to him.   Groups within the community can be distinguished, but hierarchical tendencies are resisted.   There are, for example, the itinerant prophets, who proclaim the gospel of the kingdom among Jews and gentiles, although the fundamental mission of the community is to the latter.   And there are those engaged in teaching, who, although they, too, undertake missionary activity, instruct the community in the will of God as taught by Jesus.   But whatever the contribution of the latter, when it comes to making final decisions concerning matters of doctrine and church discipline, it is the entire community, under the aegis of the exalted Son of God, that decides.

Matthew, the author of the First Gospel, lives within this community.   On behalf of his fellow believers and to meet their needs, he proclaims in written form the gospel of the kingdom.   In so doing, he holds up to them Jesus Messiah, the Son of God, as the savior of all humankind, and, in relation to Jesus, he tells them of God the Father and of what it means to be Jesus' disciple.   Although Matthew so recedes behind his document that he can scarcely be known, his gift to the church universal is one in which people in every age are called to "life."

NOTES

(Works listed in the Selected Bibliography or referred to more than once are cited by name and title only.)

1. Cf. T. Zahn, *Das Evangelium des Matthäus* (Kommentar zum Neuen Testament I: 3d ed.; Leipzig: A. Deichert, 1910); also A. Schlatter, *Der Evangelist Matthäus* (5th ed.; Stuttgart: Calwer, 1959). Although his understanding of Matthaean priority is not the same as that of Zahn and Schlatter, one might also point in this connection to the commentary by M.–J. Lagrange: *Évangile selon Saint Matthieu* (7th ed.; Paris: J. Gabalda, 1948).
2. Cf., e.g., Zahn, *Das Evangelium des Matthäus*, pp. 42–43.
3. Cf. ibid., pp. 154–59.
4. *Jesus' Proclamation of the Kingdom of God*, eds. and trs. R. H. Hiers and D. L. Holland (Lives of Jesus Series; Philadelphia: Fortress, 1971).
5. *Geschichte der Leben-Jesu-Forschung* (6th ed.; Tübingen: J. C. B. Mohr, 1951).
6. Cf. B. W. Bacon, *Studies in Matthew* (London: Constable, 1930) pp. 82, 265–335.
7. Cf. G. D. Kilpatrick, *The Origins of the Gospel according to St. Matthew* (Oxford: Clarendon, 1946) pp. 135–37.
8. Cf., e.g., G. Schille, "Bemerkungen zur Formgeschichte des Evangeliums. II. Das Evangelium des Matthäus als Katechismus," *New Testament Studies*, 4 (1957/58), 113; J. L. McKenzie, "The Gospel according to Matthew," *Jerome Biblical Commentary*, eds. R. E. Brown, J. A. Fitzmyer, and R. E. Murphy (Englewood Cliffs: Prentice Hall, 1968) pp. 62–64.
9. Cf. K. Stendahl, *The School of St. Matthew*, pp. 24–27, 29, 35.
10. Cf. W. Marxsen, *Introduction to the New Testament*, tr. G. Buswell (Philadelphia: Fortress, 1968) pp. 151–52.
11. Cf. N. Perrin, *The New Testament: An Introduction* (New York: Harcourt Brace Jovanovich, 1974) pp. 174–77.
12. Cf. W. Trilling, *Das wahre Israel* (*StANT* X; 3d ed.; Munich: Kösel, 1964), pp. 95–96, 162, 213.

13. Cf. H. Frankemölle, *Jahwebund und Kirche Christi* (*NT Abh* 10; Münster: Aschendorff, 1974), pp. 118–19, 142, 219–20, 257–61, 319–21, 358, 384–400.

14. Cf. R. Hummel, *Die Auseinandersetzung zwischen Kirche und Judentum im Matthäusevangelium* (*BEvT* 33; Munich: Kaiser, 1963), pp. 66–75, 162–73.

15. Cf. G. Strecker, *Der Weg der Gerechtigkeit* (*FRLANT* 82; Göttingen: Vandenhoeck & Ruprecht, 1962), pp. 45–49, 184–88.

16. Cf. R. Walker, *Die Heilsgeschichte im ersten Evangelium* (*FRLANT* 91; Göttingen: Vandenhoeck & Ruprecht, 1967), pp. 114–15.

17. Cf. W. G. Thompson, "An Historical Perspective in the Gospel of Matthew," *Journal of Biblical Literature*, 93 (1974) 244, 252–54, 262.

18. Cf. A. Wikenhauser, *New Testament Introduction*, tr. J. Cunningham (reprinted; New York: Herder and Herder, 1965) p. 223.

19. Cf. W. G. Kümmel, *Introduction to the New Testament*, tr. H. C. Kee (Nashville: Abingdon, 1975) pp. 57–61.

20. G. Bornkamm ("End-Expectation and Church in Matthew," *Tradition and Interpretation in Matthew*, pp. 32–33) and E. Schweizer (*Matthäus und seine Gemeinde*, p. 65) speak on this point for numerous commentators when they write, respectively: "in only a few passages does Matthew's Gospel reveal any theological reflections on the relation of these titles of honor to each other; in the first place he is satisfied with the evidence that they are all based on Scripture"; "To be sure, with Matthew neither the ecclesiology nor the christology has been systematically thought through; therefore one should not wonder if statements stand side by side which are not in complete accordance with one another."

21. For a detailed analysis of this section of the Gospel, cf. J. D. Kingsbury, *The Parables of Jesus in Matthew 13*, chaps. 2–6.

22. For a detailed analysis of the miracle-stories in Matthew's Gospel, cf. H. J. Held, "Matthew as Interpreter of the Miracle Stories," *Tradition and Interpretation in Matthew*, pp. 165–299.

23. Cf., e.g., Strecker, *Der Weg der Gerechtigkeit*, pp. 118–20, 123–26; Trilling, *Das wahre Israel*, pp. 21–51; Frankemölle, *Jahwebund und Kirche Christi*, pp. 80, 89, 144, 377, 398.

24. For a study in depth on this theme of persecution, cf. D. R. A. Hare, *The Theme of Jewish Persecution of Christians in the Gospel according to St Matthew*.

25. On the interpretation of the "parable" of the Last Judgment, cf. L. Cope, "Matthew xxv 31–46—'The Sheep and the Goats' Reinterpreted," *Novum Testamentum*, 11 (1969) 37–41.

26. Cf. Frankemölle, *Jahwebund und Kirche Christi*, chap. 1.

27. Cf., e.g., W. D. Davies, *The Sermon on the Mount* (Cambridge: Cambridge University, 1966) pp. 27–32.

28. Cf., e.g., G. Barth, "Matthew's Understanding of the Law," *Tradition and Interpretation in Matthew*, p. 94.

29. Cf. John P. Meier, "Matthew 5:17–48: Tradition and Redaction in Matthew's Gospel," unpublished doctoral dissertation, Rome, Pontifical Biblical Institute, 1975, 247–69. The bibliographical details of the published form of this dissertation can be found in the Selected Bibliography.

30. C. F. D. Moule, *The Birth of the New Testament* (Harper's New Testament Commentaries; New York: Harper & Row, 1962) p. 219.

31. Cf. Kilpatrick, *The Origins of the Gospel according to St. Matthew*, pp. 124–25.

32. Cf. Hare, *The Theme of Jewish Persecution of Christians in the Gospel according to St Matthew*, pp. 106–08, 124.

33. Cf. Kingsbury, *The Parables of Jesus in Matthew 13*, pp. 63–76.

34. Cf. W. G. Thompson, *Matthew's Advice to a Divided Community. Mt. 17, 22—18, 35*, pp. 66–68.

35. Cf., e.g., Hummel, *Die Auseinandersetzung zwischen Kirche und Judentum im Matthäusevangelium*, pp. 28–33, 159–61.

36. Cf. J. D. Kingsbury, "The Verb *Akolouthein* ("to follow") as an Index of Matthew's View of His Community," *Journal of Biblical Literature*, 97 (1978).

37. Cf. É. Cothenet, "Les prophètes chrétiens dans l'Évangile selon saint Matthieu," *L'Évangile selon Matthieu*, ed. M. Didier, 294.

38. Cf. U. Wilckens, "*Sophia*," *Theological Dictionary of the New Testament*, eds. G. Kittel and G. Friedrich (Grand Rapids: Eerdmans, 1971) VII, 505.

39. P. Hoffmann, "Der Petrus-Primat im Matthäusevangelium," *Neues Testament und Kirche*, ed. J. Gnilka (*Festschrift* R. Schnackenburg; Freiburg: Herder, 1974) pp. 94–114.

40. Cf. G. Bornkamm, "The Authority to 'Bind' and 'Loose' in the Church in Matthew's Gospel," *Jesus and Man's Hope*, ed. D. G. Buttrick (Pittsburgh: Pittsburgh Theological Seminary, 1970) I, pp. 37–50; R. E. Brown, K. P. Donfried, J. Reumann, eds., *Peter in the New Testament* (Minneapolis: Augsburg, 1973) pp. 95–101.

41. Cf. Eusebius, *Ecclesiastical History*, III. 39. 16.

42. Cf. Stendahl, *The School of St. Matthew*, pp. 30–35.

43. Cf. Strecker, *Der Weg der Gerechtigkeit*, pp. 15–35.

SELECTED BIBLIOGRAPHY

BORNKAMM, G., G. BARTH, and H. J. HELD. *Tradition and Interpretation in Matthew*, tr. P. Scott. New Testament Library. (Philadelphia: Westminster, 1963). A collection of three studies; the first shows that Matthew sees the church as oriented towards the future coming of Jesus Son of man as the Judge of all, the second deals with Matthew's understanding of the law, and the third discusses how Matthew interprets the miracle-stories of Jesus.

COPE, O. LAMAR. *Matthew: A Scribe trained for the Kingdom of Heaven.* The Catholic Biblical Quarterly Monograph Series 5. (Washington, D.C.: The Catholic Biblical Association of America, 1976). An attempt to determine, by a minute literary analysis of selected passages, how Matthew has influenced the composition of his Gospel.

DAVIES, W. D. *The Setting of the Sermon on the Mount.* (Cambridge: Cambridge University, 1964). A consideration of first-century influences, both within Judaism and the church, which led to the compilation and presentation of the moral teaching which is commonly known as the Sermon on the Mount.

GUNDRY, ROBERT H. *The Use of the Old Testament in St. Matthew's Gospel.* Supplements to Nov. Test. 18. (Leiden: E. J. Brill, 1967). An investigation of the OT quotations in Matthew's Gospel with special reference to the theme of the fulfillment of messianic prophecy.

HARE, DOUGLAS R. A. *The Theme of Jewish Persecution of Christians in the Gospel according to St Matthew.* Society for New Testament Studies Monograph Series 6. (Cambridge: Cambridge University, 1967). A treatment of the theme of Jewish persecution of Christians at the time of Matthew which aims to show how such persecution has influenced the theology of Matthew and which argues that it was directed primarily against Christian missionaries.

JOHNSON, MARSHALL D. *The Purpose of the Biblical Genealogies.* Society for New Testament Studies Monograph Series 8. (Cambridge: Cambridge University, 1969). An analysis of the genealogies of Matthew and Luke, understanding them as a form of literary expression used to articulate the conviction that Jesus is the fulfillment of the hope of Israel.

KINGSBURY, JACK DEAN. *Matthew: Structure, Christology, Kingdom.* (Philadelphia and London: Fortress and SPCK, 1975). A study of the broad structure of the First Gospel, of the titles of Majesty that together constitute Matthew's portrait of Jesus, and of his concept of the kingdom of heaven, with a view towards explaining the theology of Matthew.

————. *The Parables of Jesus in Matthew 13.* (Third reprinted edition; London and St. Louis: SPCK and Clayton Publishing House, 1976). An examination of the eight parables comprising Jesus' Parable Speech which seeks to understand the role this Speech plays within the groundplan of the First Gospel and to gain insight into both the theology of Matthew and the situation of his church.

MEIER, JOHN P. *Law and History in Matthew's Gospel.* Analecta Biblica, 71. (Rome: Biblical Institute, 1976). An attempt to plumb the meaning of the statement on the law in Matt. 5:17–20 in the light of the antitheses that follow and within the larger context of Matthew's theology of salvation-history, eschatology, and Christology.

SENIOR, DONALD P. *The Passion Narrative according to Matthew.* Bibliotheca Ephemeridum Theologicarum Lovaniensium 39. (Leuven: Leuven University, 1975). An evaluation of each distinctive feature of the passion narrative of Matthew in order to illuminate his theological perspective and redactional technique.

STENDAHL, KRISTER. *The School of St. Matthew.* (Reprinted; Philadelphia: Fortress, 1968). A discussion of the OT quotations in the First Gospel and a comparison of certain of the Gospel's literary features with the Habakkuk Commentary from Qumran leading to the thesis that Matthew's Gospel was used as a manual for teaching and administration within the church.

SUGGS, M. JACK. *Wisdom, Christology, and Law in Matthew's Gospel.* (Cambridge: Harvard University, 1970). A probe of the figure of Wisdom in Matthew's Gospel in an effort to show that Wisdom constitutes a basic part of Matthew's theology and that Matthew has identified Wisdom with Christ.

THOMPSON, WILLIAM G. *Matthew's Advice to a Divided Community: Mt. 17, 22—18, 35.* Analecta Biblica 44. (Rome: Biblical Institute, 1970). An investigation of the structure and theology of the ecclesiological discourse with special attention paid to the many literary techniques Matthew employed in composing this section.